fastread

BUYING
A HOME

**All the steps you need
to know to purchase
your dream home**

Adams Media Corporation
Avon, Massachusetts

product manager:	Gary Krebs
production director:	Susan Beale
production manager:	Michelle Roy Kelly
series designer:	Daria Perreault
layout and graphics:	Arlene Apone, Paul Beatrice, Brooke Camfield, Colleen Cunningham, Frank Rivera

Published by
Adams Media Corporation
57 Littlefield Street, Avon, MA 02322 U.S.A.
www.adamsmedia.com

ISBN: 1-58062-530-4

Printed in Canada.

J I H G F E D C B

Library of Congress Cataloging-in-Publication Data
Fastread buying a home.
p.   cm.
Includes index.
ISBN 1-58062-530-4
1. House buying--United States. 2. House buying. 3. Residental real estate--Purchasing--
United States. I. Adams Media Corporation.

HD255 .F267	2001
643'.12'0973--dc21	200103372

This publication is designed to provide accurate and authoritative information with regard to
the subject matter covered. It is sold with the understanding that the publisher is not engaged
in rendering legal, accounting, or other professional advice. If legal advice or other expert
assistance is required, the services of a competent professional person should be sought.

—From a *Declaration of Principles* jointly adopted
by a Committee of the American Bar Association
and a Committee of Publishers and Associations

Many of the designations used by manufacturers and sellers to distinguish their products are
claimed as trademarks. Where those designations appear in this book and Adams Media was
aware of a trademark claim, the designations have been printed in initial capital letters.

This book is available at quantity discounts for bulk purchases.
For information, call 1-800-872-5627.

Visit the rest of the fastread series at our web site www.adamsmedia.com

contents

introduction

Congratulations! If you are reading this book, you must be interested in buying your own home. Perhaps you will be a first-time owner and are mystified about several aspects of home buying. Or maybe it's been a few years since you had your own place, and you want to refresh your memory about the buying process.

Buying a home is likely to be one of the wisest, and most important, decisions of your life, whatever your age. Knowledge is power, so you are smart to educate yourself about what is likely to be expected of you in this area.

The biggest hurdle prospective home buyers have to face today—besides their own fears—is the down payment. Many people can afford a monthly mortgage payment, as it is likely to be about the same as or not much higher than the rent they are currently paying. But how can they come up with $10,000 or

$15,000—or even more—for that money down? If that is your concern, there are many suggestions in this book that will help you find that elusive, very large chunk of change.

Another deterrent to home buying for many renters has to do with tunnel vision. When you think of a home, do you imagine an attractive single-family house in a good neighborhood in your present community, perhaps on a half-acre lot? That narrow view of what constitutes the home you will buy could be holding you back from owning.

First home and *starter home* are terms you have probably seen frequently in those real-estate articles that have convinced you that you cannot afford a home. But look at those first words a little closer: first and starter. You are at the beginning of a long period of ownership. If you are in your 20s or 30s, you will probably own several homes in your lifetime. Even if you are older, you will, in all likelihood, move three, four, or more times.

What should you look for this time out? Forget about your dream house—that will come two or three homes down the road. First timers usually must make sacrifices—sometimes a lot of them. And forget about the house your parents live in—you are not likely to be able to begin on that level.

Try to keep your eyes on one objective: buying a solid home that you will be able to sell when you want, probably in the next few years. Your second home is likely to be more expensive, larger, or in a better neighborhood. And from that home you may move again, no doubt trading up just a little more.

Once you become a homeowner—and over time that will be an experience filled with frustration and bills and even momentary longing for the carefree days of renting—you will have realized the American dream. No matter how small the house or condominium you buy, you will, in the long run, see positive financial results.

chapter one

Where Will the Down Payment Come From?

The down payment is the one area of home buying that is likely to prove particularly challenging. You have probably given some thought to the price you want to pay, can afford to pay, or will have to pay for the home you want. Let's say you estimate the price of the home at $110,000 to $125,000. Ten percent of that is at least $11,000. Most down-payment requirements are between 10 and 20 percent of the purchase price of the home. It sounds like a lot of money—it is a lot of money! How can you put together a down payment?

Think about Your Finances

Look over your own resources that might be tapped. Maybe you are sitting on cash you had not considered. Do you have stocks to sell? Do you have a life insurance policy you can borrow against (don't forget to budget the money needed to bring its value back up again)? Do you have valuable silver or jewelry? What about tapping into retirement savings? Be careful here, though, of penalties and income taxes due on this money. Can you sell a car? One couple used their fancy foreign import, even though it was several years old, as an $18,000 down payment on a $50,000 condominium. The sellers, who were offering them a mortgage, were quite happy to take the car in lieu of cash.

In your eagerness to amass a sizable chunk of money, be careful not to leave yourself without emergency resources. Keep in mind that there are ways to buy a home with a low down payment (a discussion of which follows shortly).

If you are liquidating assets, it is best to get the money into some sort of savings account as quickly as you can. Don't wait until the day before you need a down payment to sell your Chevy!

It is not a good idea to borrow what you need as a cash advance on your credit card. Yes, you can get the money quickly without bothering relatives, and you can pay off the loan each month over a long period of time, but credit card interest rates are high and your cash advance is not tax-deductible. Consider too that if you max out your card you won't have anything available in case of an emergency, and your debt in relation to your gross monthly income might prevent you from getting a mortgage.

Are you thinking about a bank loan? Personal loans carry higher interest rates than mortgages. A personal loan will also increase your debt load in the same way borrowing on a credit card will.

Lenders often ask mortgage applicants to show proof that down-payment funds have been in a bank account for three to six months. (This is why liquidating assets should start early in your house hunting.) The lender wants to be assured that the funds have not been borrowed from another lender and that the money you have ready for the house has come from a legitimate source, such as savings or the selling of some asset (keep the receipts or statements handy).

Can Your Folks Help Out?

More than 20 percent of all first timers get some financial help from their parents or other relatives. Will the money be a loan or a gift? If it is a loan, how long do you think they can really wait before it is repaid?

If your parents can help you, the lender will probably ask them to sign a gift letter specifically stating that the money is a present and does not have to be repaid. The gift letter has to be accompanied by a document that shows Mom and Dad do indeed have the money to give, usually a bank statement.

If Mom and Dad's check represents a loan, lenders will factor in that repayment plan with your other financial obligations, and that will reduce the size of the loan they are willing to make. Indeed, some lenders will not make a loan if all of the buyer's down payment is borrowed.

Federal Government Programs

If you have exhausted your own resources and still need money, maybe you can turn to a government-backed home-buying program that calls for lower than normal down payments. The Federal Housing Administration (FHA) is a government agency under the umbrella of the U.S. Department of Housing and Urban Development (HUD).

With an FHA-backed loan, you can buy with a down payment of less than 3 percent. However, you will be required to pay their mortgage insurance, and that will probably cost you 3.8 percent of the loan up front (it can be financed) and annual payments of 0.5 percent. Private mortgage insurance with conventional loans (covered later in this chapter) also calls for a monthly charge to the home buyer, but there is no up-front fee. If you get a gift from a relative (or anyone else) toward your down payment, under FHA rules that gift can even extend to covering your closing costs. For more information about FHA loans, call (800) 225-5342.

If you qualify for a loan from the Veterans' Administration (VA), you do not have to make any down payment. These loans are available to veterans or widows or widowers of veterans who died of service-related injuries. Closing costs can be covered by a gift here, too.

The Farmers Home Administration (FmHA) is not a household name, but it can make a homeowner of you. If you are looking to buy in a rural area, the FmHA offers no-down-payment programs and lower than market interest rates. Here's the catch: The house must meet their definition of rural and must be your principal residence.

Look to Your State

Every state offers some type of home-buying program for first timers that features low down-payment requirements and lower than market interest rates. Money is available through bond programs, with a quasi-autonomous agency handling the program known as a mortgage finance agency or housing finance authority or some similar name.

There may be an income ceiling for those wishing to buy, and you will likely to be restricted to certain areas of some towns—and not any block in town either. But the program works!

It is only for first-time buyers or those who have not owned a home for a specified number of years, usually three to five.

Private Mortgage Insurance (PMI)

Private Mortgage Insurance is a common expense for first-time buyers. Lenders usually require PMI of borrowers who need 90 percent financing, virtually all of those who want 95 percent, and sometimes even those applying for 80 percent loans.

Rates vary from one insurance lender to another, so shop around. You don't have to come up with the whole amount at the closing. It's a one-time payment, borrowed at the closing, and then repaid monthly or annually. Interest is tax deductible.

When you are in your home for a few years and after your equity reaches a certain percentage—usually 20 percent—you are entitled to cancel your PMI policy. However, you must keep after the lender about this. Many homeowners do not know this policy can be done away with at some point and are needlessly paying premiums well after they no longer need that insurance.

A Lease/Purchase Program

While a developer can offer a lease/purchase plan to a buyer, more often it is the seller who accepts this plan. Here is how the plan works, although there can be any number of variations. You rent a house or condominium, signing a contract that states that at the end of 6, 12, or 18 months you will be allowed to buy that property, at a price set at the signing of the contract. This contract protects you from ordinary price increases in the housing market each year. Another good feature is that the sellers, who for the moment will be your landlords, allow you to apply some of your rent toward the purchase, and that amount will go toward your down payment.

Try to negotiate as much as possible of that rent toward your down payment. If the owner offers 20 percent, try for 50 or even 100 percent of it.

The lease/purchase plan can work well with new-home developers who are anxious to sell their properties and do not mind renting them initially, with the proviso that the tenant plans to buy. You should know here that your option money will not be refunded if you elect not to buy at the end of the specified time. Unless you can prove some sort of fraud on the part of the seller, you do not have any legal grounds for getting that money back. It must be applied toward the purchase of the house. If the real-estate market goes down, you can, of course, decline to exercise your option to buy, a move that could be wise over the long term, even though it means forfeiting the option money.

The Sellers

They, too, could offer you a low down payment along with a mortgage, but it would have to be in their interests. There is more about seller financing coming up in the next chapter.

Equity Sharing

Whether you will find equity sharing workable depends on the state of the real-estate market where you intend to buy and on the national economy (and on whether anyone in your area has heard of equity sharing). You also need an investor, and no outsider is likely to want to buy without knowing whether the value of your home will increase regularly. But a family member may be willing to join you. Mom and Dad, for example, are more likely to tolerate little or no return on their investment.

Shared equity deals can be arranged in a number of ways. Most commonly, an investor (known as the owner-investor) provides the down payment and even the closing costs. The buyer (known as the owner-occupant) lives in the home, makes the monthly mortgage payments, and pays for taxes and maintenance. Both names are on the mortgage and on the deed.

At the end of a specified period, usually five years, the home is sold. The owner-investor receives the original down payment and any closing costs he or she paid from the proceeds of the sale. If there is a profit, the two split it. If the owner-occupant wants to continue living in that house, he or she can refinance the loan as sole buyer.

Some lenders take a dim view of equity sharing. If they go along with the plan, they will probably demand a high down payment, perhaps even 25 percent. Some will require that the owner-occupant's income be the only income to qualify for the loan. Previously, many lenders had used the combined incomes of the investor and occupant to determine qualification. You may also find you will be quoted a higher interest rate and might have to pay points (a point is 1 percent) on your loan.

What's That—No Down Payment?

A few builders from time to time offer "no money down" programs, many of which come with higher-than-market interest rates and loan fees (points). You are likely to have to pay private mortgage insurance, too. Also, the programs might be difficult to qualify for, calling for excellent credit and a large amount in savings.

Do some homework here. You might be able to do far better with a low down-payment home and no loan fees or a better interest rate. Or you might want to wait a while and continue to save until you have more for a down payment. Remember, if it sounds too good to be true, it is. No one—neither the builder nor the lender—is going to take much of a chance with this program. Those higher charges are their safety net—and your expense.

One final note: Be aware of the real-estate market, both nationally and locally, when you are ready to buy so that you know whether you are operating from a position of strength in a buyers' market or whether at the moment the power is with the seller. The market will affect how much you will have to come up with for your home.

chapter two

Choosing the Right Mortgage for You

It is wise not to begin serious house hunting until you know about mortgages and, in fact, have been preapproved by a mortgage lender. Indeed, most real-estate agents will hustle you off to a lender before showing you homes.

Preapproved or Prequalified

A few years ago, if you were prequalified for a mortgage, that was considered novel and quite beneficial for home shopping. Now, real-estate agents prefer seeing preapproved house hunters coming into their offices, and sellers are happier greeting those would-be buyers, too.

What's the difference? You can be prequalified simply with a phone call to a mortgage lender. The loan officer will ask your income, a general figure for the amount of your debt, quickly run some numbers, and tell you the amount that institution would likely lend you for a mortgage, based on your replies.

To be preapproved requires a good deal more effort on both the borrower's and the lender's sides. You apply for a mortgage, as if you have already chosen the house you want. The lender weighs your qualifications, checking your income, your debt, and your credit report. He or she will ask for pay stubs, bank statements, and go through the whole application process.

After reviewing your application and approving what it sees, the lending institution issues a letter or certificate saying that you have been preapproved for a loan of a certain size. All that is missing is the appraisal by the lender, and that takes place after you have found the home you want to buy. The lender will also want to be sure that your income situation has not changed since you were preapproved.

Generally speaking, being preapproved does not guarantee that you will get a specific interest rate. But if you are concerned about rates rising at the time you are house hunting, look for a lender who will lock in your rate for at least 60 days.

It makes sense to begin house hunting after you either have a preapproved mortgage or are 99.9 percent certain of getting one. After your loan is preapproved, you will know exactly how much of a mortgage you can get and, given your down payment, in what price range you should be looking. If you want a house more costly than the mortgage allowed, you will have to come up with a larger down payment to fill the dollar gap between the mortgage amount and the sale price.

Who Offers Mortgages?

It will pay you—perhaps thousands of dollars over the life of the loan—to shop around for mortgage terms. They are not the same with every institution. You might want to start with the bank that has your savings and/or checking accounts, though; lenders often give preferential treatment to their long-time customers. Other sources include savings banks and savings and loan associations, commercial banks, credit unions, mortgage bankers, mortgage brokers, government agencies, and seller financing.

Mortgage bankers are companies that qualify applicants, find the best available loans, fund the initial loan, and then sell or place that loan with another lender or investor. Mortgage brokers are persons (or companies) who, for a fee, will find house hunters a lender somewhere around the country.

Government agencies that lend mortgage money include the Federal Housing Administration (FHA), the Federal Department of Veterans' Administration (VA), the Federal Farmers Home Administration (FmHA), and your state's Mortgage Finance Agency.

In seller financing, home sellers offer mortgages to buyers, usually for a limited time of three to five years, after which the buyer secures more traditional, long-term financing. Seller financing works for buyers in a very slow sellers' market, in which property after property remains unsold for months, perhaps years, or when a seller is particularly eager to move right away and cannot wait a few months while his house goes through the ordinary selling channels. This can be an excellent deal for the seller who does not need the house proceeds immediately and sees that quite a nice return can be realized by offering a loan to the buyer at 8 or 9 percent interest.

Your Loan Choices

Lenders may have several loan packages, with differences in length of the loan, interest rate, and other particulars. However, the two most conventional loans are the fixed-rate mortgage (for 15, 20, 25, or 30 years) and the adjustable-rate mortgage (ARM). ARMs offer a "teaser" low-interest rate at the outset of the loan that can be three or more points lower than a fixed-rate loan, but that figure can rise dramatically after the first year, and steadily thereafter.

Interest rates that lenders charge for ARMs are pegged to an independent financial index. There are many choices of index here, carrying a variety of components. To protect home buyers from large rate increases, most lenders set limits on the amount rates may fluctuate when it is time for a loan's interest rate to be determined. This is known as the adjustable rate cap. With a lifetime cap, lenders set a ceiling and floor for rate increases and decreases over the life of an ARM. The lifetime cap is expressed either as a particular percentage rate or as five to seven percentage points over or under that initial rate. Be sure to ask about caps when you inquire about ARMs.

Some borrowers these days are opting for 15-year loans in place of the more traditional 30-year term, both to build equity faster and to save thousands of dollars in finance charges. These loans are a little harder to secure than the 30-year terms because the monthly payments are higher, which translates into your having to earn more money to qualify. Your payments with a 15-year mortgage are 20 to 30 percent above that of a 30-year mortgage because more of each monthly payment goes toward principal and not interest.

You may also come upon balloon mortgages. When you take on a balloon loan, you agree to make a fixed monthly payment that will amortize your loan over, say, 30 years. You might pay interest only on the loan, but then on a specified date—5, 7, 10, or any predetermined number of years in the future—the entire unpaid balance of the loan becomes due and payable. You must pay up, refinance, or lose the property.

Which Type of Loan Is Best for You?

Balloon mortgages can keep monthly housing costs down if you are certain of a company transfer—or plan to move for any other reason—well within the period of the balloon. Otherwise, be wary when you see the words *balloon payment*. Similarly, if you plan to pull up stakes after just three or four years, you might want to choose the attractive initial rates of the ARM.

If you intend to stay in the house for an indeterminate number of years, but certainly more than three or five, and if interest rates are low at the moment, your choice should probably be the fixed-rate loan.

What to Ask Lenders

Now that you are familiar with what is out there in terms of mortgages, you are ready to start calling mortgage lenders. When you call potential lenders, have a list of questions written out and by your side. Ask for the mortgage department or a mortgage loan officer. Following are the questions that should be addressed:

- What types of financing do you have available now? Does the lender offer both fixed-rate and adjustable plans? Are FHA and VA mortgages available? What other plans does that particular institution offer?
- How long a term are you willing to offer for each type of loan? Find out whether the term is fixed on adjustable-rate loans and whether there is a lower rate of interest for shorter-term loans.
- Can ARMs be converted to fixed-rate loans at some point? You might want to convert over the course of your loan. If it can be done, what is the cost?
- What guidelines do you use for loan qualifications?

- What is your minimum down-payment requirement for each type of loan?
- Do you charge points?
- Is there a loan origination fee?
- Is there an application fee? How much? Remember, this is a nonrefundable charge and cannot be applied to any other expense.
- Can you give a rough estimate of closing costs in relation to the percentage of the home's sale price?
- Is there a prepayment penalty on any of the loans? This is important if you think you might be transferred and thus have to move sooner than you plan to right now.
- Do you offer preferred customer benefits? Some lenders lower the interest rates on mortgage loans if the borrower makes use of the bank's other services.
- How long will a mortgage decision take after an application is made?
- How long will a mortgage commitment remain effective? Some lenders will make a commitment for 90 days, with renewals available. Some will make commitments for up to six months, especially on new construction.
- Does the interest rate remain constant on the loan commitment? Some lenders will commit to a loan at the interest rate prevailing at the time of closing, which can be risky for you in a time of fluctuating rates. Other lenders will guarantee the rate but will hold you to that rate even if rates go down before you close. Look for lenders that will guarantee the best rate.
- What's new? Many lenders inaugurate special mortgage plans for that institution only. Ask if that lender has any new mortgage programs on the horizon.

Talk with four to six lenders. Ask to lock in the rate you want. Also, be sure you are getting comparative quotes on the same loans. For example, you might be given one quote on a 30-year, fixed-rate loan. But this might really mean that the lender offers a 30-year loan with a fixed rate for the first seven years, with a lower interest rate for those seven years. Then, there will be a balloon payment or refinancing at prevailing rates due at the end of that time for the final 23 years.

How Much Can You Borrow?

Mortgage lenders will only lend you what they feel you can afford. For example, if they are willing to offer you a mortgage for $110,000 and you need $130,000 for the home you want, you will have to make up the difference by coming up with another $20,000 for the down payment.

Ten or 15 years ago, most lenders would go by the gross annual income formula. If you made $30,000 a year, you could get a mortgage loan of $60,000. Today, lenders who still use that formula—and they are mostly small, hometown institutions—allow two and a half or even three times gross annual income.

Using the income to housing costs formula, the anticipated housing expenses are computed. These expenses include mortgage payment, real-estate taxes, fire and catastrophe insurance, and mortgage insurance, if any. To qualify with many lenders, your total monthly figure for housing expenses must not exceed 28 percent of your gross monthly income (some lenders will go slightly higher).

Another criterion is the income to long-term debt payment formula. Here all of the borrower's long-term (10 months or more) debt payments are calculated, including car payments, large outstanding charge account balances, child support, and college loans.

To qualify with most lenders, the total monthly payment for housing expenses and long-term debts should not exceed 33 to 36 percent of gross monthly income.

Preparing to Apply for a Loan

Mortgage lenders are in the business of lending money for mortgages. They want to help you. In certain economies, they are even dying to lend money.

Having a document from a lender stating that that institution will offer you a mortgage of X dollars will make you look like the serious buyer you are. It's also a good negotiating tool; no eager seller is going to quickly turn away a qualified buyer.

There are many factors, as you will see, that enter into being approved for a home loan. Some you cannot change, but others you can change (legally) to make yourself look good—or at least better.

The Paper Chase

Income, debt, down payment, and a good credit report are the prime components lenders use as a gauge of creditworthiness. From that information, they will come up with an amount they are willing to lend you. You might learn that you need to pay off some old bills, clean up your credit, or save still more. Whatever lenders pass on to you in the way of tips will help move you along through the mortgage approval process.

You will most likely need the following information to start this process:

- *Address(es)*—where you have lived for the past two years.

- *List of assets*—holdings such as stocks and bonds, IRAs, vested amounts in retirement plans, surrender value of life insurance policies, cars, and so on. List current balances, names and addresses of institutions, and account numbers for each item.
- *List of debts*—credit cards, auto loans, school loans, and other debts. Show the names of the organizations that have extended credit to you, the addresses, your account numbers, the amounts owed, and the monthly payments. Pay off as many bills as possible to reduce your debt load.
- *Marital status*
- *Extra income*—regular sources of extra income, not the occasional overtime.
- *Foreclosure and bankruptcy*—must be reported if you experienced either within the previous 10 years.
- *Gift letter*—if Mom and Dad have helped you with the down payment. Be sure to have a letter from them attesting that they do not expect to be repaid.
- *Income and employment records*—W-2 statements for the last two years and pay stubs from the previous month. If you are self-employed, you will need to show your federal tax returns for the two previous years as verification of income.
- *Social security number*
- *VA documentation*—contact your local VA office six to eight weeks before applying for a loan for a certificate of eligibility.

Your Credit Report

A vitally important part of your loan approval is your credit report. It is wise to send for a copy now, before a lender sees it, so that you can clear up any errors.

There are three national credit bureaus you can call to get a report: Equifax (800) 685-1111, Experian (800) 682-7654, and Trans Union (216) 779-7200. Each charges about $8 for a copy of a single credit report and $16 for a couple's joint report.

In this document, you will find your personal credit history, including when and how promptly you have paid credit cards, department store charges, auto loans, and the like. This is not, as many consumers mistakenly believe, a rating service. Credit bureaus attach no rating to those they list; they merely collect data and pass it on upon request.

Go over everything in that report carefully. If you see an account in which a payment has not been recorded, bring along with you to the mortgage loan officer a copy of your canceled check to that store or credit card company. If you find an outright mistake in your report, write to the source of the erroneous data and clear up the matter with them. Work with the credit bureau until you are satisfied that the mistake has been corrected.

Give yourself plenty of time. Credit bureaus can work slowly. Allow at least a month or two between securing your report and approaching a lender. You never know what you will find in that document, no matter how religiously you have paid your bills.

Dealing with a Poor Credit History, Including Bankruptcy

Maybe you know that your credit report is going to be a mess. Now what do you do?

Be prepared. Were you delinquent in paying bills for four months in 1995 because you had just been laid off? Because you had serious surgery? You can send a letter of explanation to the credit bureau and ask them to affix it to your report to serve as an explanation for anyone requesting your file. Be ready to offer that explanation to the mortgage loan officer as well so that he or she is prepared for the bad news. Copies of doctors' bills can help document long illnesses. If you had a dispute with a credit card company over a payment that is still being worked out in correspondence, bring copies of those letters with you to the lender.

If you have no explanation for the six months or one year or two years of late payments, offer to make a larger down payment than would normally be required. Or, you might suggest a pledged account. This means the lending institution will have extra collateral available in a third-party escrow account in case of your nonpayment. Funds supplied by you equal to three or four months of your mortgage payment are placed in the account. This can be done by the seller or any other third party to the sale, such as a title company—maybe even your employer if you do not mind going outside your immediate circle.

There are ways that borrowers with less than a spotless credit record can become homeowners, even though creditworthiness is one of the principal criteria for securing a mortgage. You have several options:

- *Mortgage brokers.* A mortgage broker is helpful for buyers with less than perfect credit histories.
- *Seller's mortgage.* This is offered by the seller of the home for a term of three years or so, after which you secure a mortgage.
- *Assumable loans.* This means taking over someone else's mortgage, such as those offered by the FHA and VA, often with no need to qualify on your own. Adjustable-rate loans can be assumed, but, generally, fixed-rate loans cannot be assumed.
- *Lease/purchase.* (See Chapter 1.)
- *Cosigner.* Parents or another family member might cosign your mortgage, thereby increasing the likelihood that your application will be approved.

Bankruptcy

Bankruptcy is more serious than late payments. If you can afford to buy a home now, however, do not let that credit blot keep you from approaching mortgage loan officers. There are, legally, no time limits on how soon you can secure a conventional mortgage after a bankruptcy is discharged, although some lenders will turn you down no matter how far back the bankruptcy occurred. With FHA-insured loans, a bankruptcy must be discharged for at least one year; the Department of Veterans Affairs insists on a two-year wait with VA loans.

chapter three

Buying Solo or with Others

How you buy your home—how you hold title to that house or apartment—is important to your enjoyment of that property and to your financial life.

Single and House Hunting

There is an irony here that—if you are old enough—may not have escaped you. Roughly 20 years ago, young single people began to purchase homes. They did not wait until they were married, they did not wait to buy with a "significant other," and they did not wait until they turned 40. If they could afford a house or condominium and it made good financial sense for them to buy, they did so, even if they were 25 years old.

However, in the space of that 20 years, the price of homes has risen drastically, and so have down-payment requirements. Now, many would-be buyers seem to be thrown back to the years before the early 1970s. It is not being single that is hurting them. What often does them in is the need for two incomes to swing the expense.

While many single buyers might well be able to carry a mortgage payment, there often remains the giant hurdle of the down payment. And, again, there is no second income to toss into the pot.

All Together Now

There are single parents who join forces and buy together, brothers and sisters who buy and share houses, and former college roommates who take the plunge and sign for mortgages not long after graduating and starting their first jobs. Each of these new homeowners has been imaginative enough to see beyond the strictly traditional and say "Why not?" to carving out his or her own interpretation of homeowning. Each has been clever enough to see that owning a portion of a house is still better, financially, than renting. They also realize that a share in a house today can turn into sole ownership of the next place and the one after that. Stretch your thinking and this might work for you. Following are some additional points to consider.

Why *not* buy half a house? That shared-housing style is solid and well conceived, and it is not just for those 25-year-olds. Many strapped renters can enter into one of these buying arrangements at any age and can enjoy the privacy, freedom, investment potential, and tax advantages of ownership.

You and another buyer could purchase a two-family house, each living in one apartment. Or you could buy a single-family house, sharing it equally or spending money to convert it into two complete dwelling units. Yes, you will essentially be living in an

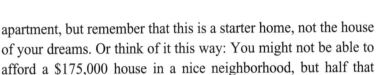

apartment, but remember that this is a starter home, not the house of your dreams. Or think of it this way: You might not be able to afford a $175,000 house in a nice neighborhood, but half that house at $87,500 could be well within your means.

In the early and mid-1980s, there was a home style put up by a few developers known as "mingles" housing. These were homes built specifically for sharing and were often constructed in high-priced areas, particularly resorts, where the cost of a single-family home would be prohibitive to many buyers. There was a common living/dining area, a kitchen, and then separate bedrooms and baths at each end of the dwelling. For whatever reason, mingles housing has not exactly grown at a furious pace. But if you find some of these homes in your area, it might pay to investigate them. Call your local or statewide builders' association and ask where there might be some developments.

If you cannot find any, look at traditional new construction that lends itself nicely to sharing. These homes will have a kitchen, a large living/dining area, a master bedroom/bath at one side of the house, and another bedroom and bath or two at the opposite end. That design works better for unrelated sharers than having all of the bedrooms clustered at one end of the house.

"Put it in writing" is the cardinal rule for sharing ownership of a house. Have a lawyer draw up an agreement for the two (or more) of you, covering every aspect of your buying, maintaining, and selling of that home.

How will you legally hold title to such a house? Your options are spelled out later in this chapter.

Do not buy with others without knowing fully the financial situation of your prospective house sharer(s). These arrangements work better if everyone involved has similar incomes and assets. You do not want to end up toting most of the financial load because your sharer lost his minimum-wage job and your income as a controller is now expected to carry the house.

How You Will Own Your Home

Owning a house, as you already know, is an enormous responsibility. The key word here is *owning*. The names on the deed to a property are accountable for that piece of real estate—to the mortgage holder, to the insurance company, to the local tax office and utilities, and to some degree, even to the neighbors, for keeping up the appearance of the place. Despite that burden, the house is an asset—an important part of one's estate—that is passed on to the person(s) designated in a will.

If you are single, you are likely to have that house in "sole ownership," which means you are the only title holder. (You could also take the title in a living trust. Your attorney can explain the benefits there.) When there is more than one owner involved, even if the two owners are married to each other, there can be questions about inheritance and tax consequences of the ownership style they have chosen.

At this stage, everyone involved in a joint purchase should be deciding how they want to buy so that any problems that surface can be worked out. Let's start with the most common buying style.

Married Couples

"Well, naturally we're buying together," you say. "We'll own the house equally." Of course, what could be simpler? That way when one dies, the property automatically passes to the other, without having to go through probate.

This ownership style is know as "joint tenants with right of survivorship." When one party dies, usually only a certified copy of the death certificate and an affidavit of survivorship need to be recorded, and then the name of the deceased is cleared from the title to that property.

But just a minute. While that is the usual way a husband and wife own property, it is not necessarily their best choice. By holding a property jointly, some couples raise the likelihood that the IRS could take a bigger chunk of their wealth than necessary in estate taxes. Also, in some marriages, buyers might want to leave their share of the house to their children from a previous union. In such cases, owning as joint tenants probably would not be the best choice.

There is an alternative to the joint tenants buying style. "Tenants in common" allows each spouse to co-own a property, but each can leave his or her share to anyone he or she chooses, not necessarily the spouse.

In community property states (Arizona, California, Idaho, Louisiana, Nevada, New Mexico, Texas, Washington, and Wisconsin), spouses can hold title as community property. Each then owns one half of the property, and that half can be passed on upon death by will.

A major, major point to keep in mind here is that joint tenancy with right of survivorship overrides both a will and a prenuptial agreement. So, if Karen marries Joe and the two have a prenup in which Karen leaves her share of the house to the children from her first marriage, but the two buy that property in joint tenancy, then upon Karen's death, her share of the house automatically becomes Joe's.

Couples Living Together

Opposite-sex couples who purchase a home together need to work out every detail of that purchase. This situation calls for a contract, along with deciding ownership style. When co-owners are not married, the issues become more complex, such as who will maintain the property, what happens when one party wants to sell, and who will inherit a co-owner's share upon his or her death.

There is no law requiring unmarried sharers to have a written agreement, but it is a wise step to take. A written contract is not really a prenuptial agreement. It does not cover all financial aspects of the sharers' lives, only that of shared housing. A true prenup goes into everything.

The legal system sometimes has its hands full with couples living together. Cohabitation is still illegal in a handful of states, although those particular laws are rarely enforced. However, there is little uniformity among the other states regarding the legal status of the millions of couples who live together. This legal area continues to change.

Such relationships are governed by contract law. When problems arise, they might be decided by a jury in civil court rather than by a family-court judge.

The living-together phrase usually applies to opposite sex couples. But same-sex couples who live together have similar concerns in owning property.

Single people in any long-term relationship may want to pass the property they co-own to each other. Or they might want to will their share to a designated family member.

Most unmarried couples own their homes, in equal or unequal interests, as tenants in common. But here is an example of how this can sometimes cause complications. Frank wills his share of the house he shares with Jeff to his 24-year-old daughter, Kate, who lives 2,000 miles away. What is Kate to do with the house? She hardly knows the 42-year-old Jeff. Her options are to sell her share to Jeff; to rent her share, with Jeff approving of the tenant; or to sell the house with Jeff, with the two splitting any profit. Here is a perfect example of the need for a contract between co-owners, spelling out every possibility as it applies to them and the property.

Besides a strong contract, you should also keep careful records of all major expenditures and purchases made while you are together. Yes, this is unromantic, and it may seem petty, but when love flies out the window, it is amazing how important money, assets, and estates become.

Naturally, any contract should be in writing. Courts refuse to "assume" partners' understandings by their words or actions. The agreement can be worked out just between partners or with the help of a lawyer. As you read in earlier examples, the contract will cover how the home is owned, what will happen in the event the two separate—whether the house will be sold then or at any specified time—and how the proceeds from a sale will be split. There can be clauses covering any decision about the termination of the agreement—such as *upon the death of one partner*, *upon marriage to each other*, or *upon marriage to someone else*—or just a mutual agreement in writing about termination. Actually, a contract can contain as many stipulations as the parties choose, about any aspect of owning and maintaining the property.

Are these contracts enforceable? Well, they can be challenged, like any other contract, but a well-written agreement can protect partners. Anything in writing is stronger than one half of a now-defunct couple appearing in court and merely saying, "He promised me we'd sell the condo in four years."

A Living Trust

A growing number of Americans, seeking to avoid probate and its attendant costs, have instituted a living trust instead of a will (sometimes along with a will). Both sole owners and co-owners can hold title to a home in a living trust. Among other provisions, this allows for automatic property disposition upon death, according to the trust terms, without delays or probate costs.

Until death, the property owner retains complete control over the living trust property, as its trustor, trustee, and beneficiary.

When that trustor dies, the trust assets automatically pass according to its terms, to the person(s) designated.

During the trustor's life, the living trust can be changed and the properties in that trust can be bought, sold, and refinanced the way they would be if there were no trust.

Whether you are no-strings unattached, married, or in a committed relationship, you will no doubt want to see a lawyer and/or your accountant to discuss the ramifications of various types of property ownership as they affect your estate.

Buying with Cousins, Friends, or Coworkers

In this situation, you will almost certainly want to purchase a home as "tenants in common," although you might also consider forming a partnership, particularly if there are more than two of you who want to co-own a property. Your accountant can help you choose what is best for all of you.

Finally, you might also specify in any contract that any disputes you both (or all) cannot resolve will be turned over to the American Arbitration Association for settlement. Sometimes only a qualified outsider can come up with a solution to a heated disagreement.

chapter four

Location, Location, Location: Choosing the Right Neighborhood or Town

The most important factor in smart home buying is location. Location is your lot, the neighborhood around it, and the town in which the neighborhood lies. Location will make a difference in the size of your property tax bill, the quality of schools, and probably how long you will stay in that house. It will certainly make a difference in whether you profit from its sale. Real-estate agents and everyone else engaged in buying and selling homes agree that new homes are not necessarily better buys than older houses. What determines the value of each, they say, is that most important factor: location.

If you purchase the most modest house in a high-priced community, you can do very well indeed for yourself, investment-wise. The more expensive houses will lift yours to a higher level than it would command in lesser neighborhoods. You have an equally sound investment if your home is in the same price range as the ones around it. But if you buy what you consider an attractive house that happens to be in a bad neighborhood, you might just as well toss your potential investment out in a plastic trash bag. Location is that important.

Tips for Scouting Locations

You may not be able to afford the very best house and location, but knowing why one location is more valuable than another will help you get the most for the money you can afford to spend. Here are a few general tips to keep in mind:

- Stay away from a community with too many "For Sale" signs. Perhaps the only corporation in the area is relocating. Too much competition, with too many houses or condos on the market, drives down the value of each property. If you can see no apparent reason for so many signs, it would be wise to head for the town hall to see what is on the books for that part of town.
- Avoid the house that has been over-improved for its block. You do not want the highest-priced house in the neighborhood. You will never get your money back when it is your turn to sell.
- Look for a house that is traditional for its neighborhood. A California ultracontemporary home in a community of two-story colonials could bring you problems when you want to sell, if you cannot find others who share your enthusiasm for alternative architecture.
- If you think you might be moving again in just a few years, buy the most ordinary home or condo you can find, one that can easily satisfy the greatest number of house seekers when you do decide to sell. This has long been a

successful buying strategy for corporate transferees and military families.

- Check into commuting time, schools, houses of worship, and nearby shopping.
- Ask the seller, or the real-estate agent, about any extra fees. Besides real-estate taxes, there can be costs for trash pickup or curbside recycling, as well as fees for mandatory membership in a community or condo association.
- Be very sure that if you want to make any drastic changes to the appearance of the house or condo that the zoning laws or condo association will permit you to do so. Zoning laws could apply to building a sunroom/greenhouse, constructing an extra bedroom, putting in an in-ground pool, and even building a sturdy tool shed. Don't laugh at the latter. Some towns have made owners take down children's tree houses because they violated zoning laws!
- Talk with the neighbors. The very best way to learn about a neighborhood is to talk to its residents.

Choosing the Right Town

If you have not decided exactly where to look for a home, whether within a 20-mile radius of where you are now or 2,700 miles away, there are some factors that apply in choosing any community.

Taxes

Property taxes are formulated in two ways: mill rate and assessed valuation. A mill is one-tenth of one cent. It is the actual dollar figure you pay on each $1,000 of the assessed value of your property. So, if your home is assessed at $100,000 and your town's mill rate is 23.7, then you must pay $23.70 for each $1,000 of assessed value.

But finding the town with the lowest mill rate will not bring you the lowest property taxes. Not every town bases its mill rate on an assessment of 100 percent of fair market value. Town A might have a mill rate of 23.7 on 60 percent of fair market value assessment, while Town B has the same mill rate on 100 percent of fair market value.

Call the town collector's office or ask your real-estate agent for tax structure information on the towns that interest you. If you should discover that the low taxes of a particular community are based upon an evaluation done 10 years or more ago, be wary. Another assessment may be in the works, and you may face a significant jump in taxes soon after you buy a house there.

Residential taxes are not, of course, the only source of revenue for a municipality. Income is also generated by taxes on business and industrial property. A town with a high proportion of both is, therefore, likely to have a lower overall tax rate, since taxes upon the nonresidential structures help to offset the cost of services to community residents.

Following are some points to consider:

- Is the town about to undergo a re-evaluation of its property taxes? It is certainly rare for taxes to go down in such situations.
- How does the present and projected school population relate to the school plant facilities in the town? Will the town need more teachers or even a new school (or a few new schools) in the near future?
- How much open space exists? How is it zoned? More new housing, of any kind, can increase the school population and the demand for municipal services, like new roads, more than the added tax dollars they generate—thus, higher taxes for everyone. On the other hand, new office

buildings, industrial parks, shopping centers, and the like can cushion the tax demand on individuals.

- What shape are the town buildings and equipment in? A new town hall, a new police station, or new police cars and fire engines can cost plenty.
- How has the town dealt with taxes over the years? Have rates been relatively stable? Is the town financially healthy?

Schools

Schools can have a serious impact on the taxes you pay. Also, when it is time to sell the home you are buying now, many buyers are likely to be interested in the schools.

Consider the following:

- How many elementary schools are there in town?
- Are the children bussed?
- How are the grades grouped?
- What is the average class size in elementary school? What special programs are offered?
- What subjects do junior high or middle school students study? At what grade can foreign language study begin? Are there advanced math courses for bright students below the high school level?
- What about computers? Are they in the high school? At what computer-to-student ratio?
- How do local pupils rate on standardized tests against other area towns or other parts of the state or the nation?
- What courses are offered at the high school level? What courses are required for graduation?
- What percentage of each high school class graduates?
- What do seniors do after graduation? What percentage goes on to college? Which colleges? Professional training schools?

If schools rank high on your list of considerations, take the time to visit several schools in that town before you make a commitment to buy a home. Principals are usually happy to discuss their schools and programs with the parents of prospective students.

Services

Learn about the services that are available in the community you are considering. Here are some you should consider:

- *Refuse collection.* Some towns provide it; others do not.
- *Sewers.* Large cities use sewers, and rural areas use septic tanks. In the suburbs, you may find both in the same town. Is there a sewer use fee? If so, add it to your taxes.
- *Water.* Is city water free (included in your property tax bill), or do you pay the city separately for the water you use? Do you pay a private water company? If your property uses well water, is the water pure and plentiful?
- *Road service.* How well will your streets be plowed in winter? Sometimes you can get a clue by how well they are maintained during the fall "leaf pick-up" season and by how well they are maintained when it comes to potholes.
- *Police protection.* What is the crime rate like? Can you go out safely at night? Are break-ins common? Does the town maintain rescue vehicles, or must you pay for private ambulance services? How large is the police force in relation to the population? How does this compare with other areas? You can learn all of this from a phone call to the community relations department of the local police force.
- *Fire department.* Is the fire department full time or volunteer? How well are they equipped? Is equipment paid for by taxes or by contributions?

- *Library services.* How large is the library system in relation to the town? Does it belong to an interlibrary exchange group so that books can be borrowed from other branches? Does it feature any special collections? Is there a solid children's department?
- *Social services.* Does the town sponsor programs for senior citizens, teenagers, and children? Are family counseling services available?
- *Recreation.* If recreation and cultural facilities are high on your list of must-haves, you would be wise to look into what your town has to offer.
- *Accessibility to work.* How far are you willing to travel, twice a day, five days a week, in order to get to and from work?

A Look at a Lot

It is best not to decide you want to buy a house without first giving careful attention to the lot on which it is situated. You may think that while the house is eye-catching, the lot is just ground. However, you should be aware of the importance of that piece of earth, too. Here are some points to weigh.

Shape

Generally, rectangular or square lots with good frontage on the road and good depth behind the house are best. Pie shapes, triangles, and multi-angles always require explanations and usually hurt resale value.

Size

A quarter of an acre is a large lot in a city; an acre is the norm for more expensive housing in the suburbs. Large pieces of property that cannot be subdivided rarely add to the value of a house. For example, that handsome Tudor home on Summit Lane would sell for $265,000 on a half acre, since all of its neighbors have half acres. The fact that it has seven acres of land fanning out behind it and its neighbors on both sides, some of which is swamp and some rock and virtually undevelopable, will not increase the resale value of the Tudor by a penny. It may, in fact, hinder resale, since the owners are paying property taxes on all that land.

Contour

Level land is best. Houses built on steep slopes are often hard to sell. Buyers are especially wary of houses built below the level of the road, where driveways slope sharply downward. When choosing your lot and/or home, be aware of the area's contour as well as your particular lot's contour. Flood plain maps made by the U.S. government are available in many town halls and will show you the contour of the land throughout the town. Some parts of town may be considered flood prone; homeowners in these areas may be required to carry flood insurance.

What is beneath the grass? Could there once have been a garbage dump there? A forest? A swamp? These become essential questions prior to purchase if you are considering a house that uses a septic tank for waste disposal, since the composition of the earth will determine how well that tank and its lines will drain. Especially poor drainage could mean a non-working system, which taken to its farthest limit could mean an uninhabitable house.

What is underground will also affect house settling. Houses built on rock will settle little. Those built upon landfill may settle unevenly, especially if the fill consists of tree trunks and other debris collected as a development was cleared and constructed. As a general rule of thumb, choose high ground if you can.

Position

Corner lots, the most desirable location for business, are usually not that desirable in residential real estate. They are too exposed and require trees or fencing for privacy. Cul-de-sacs are popular with families with young children and are especially salable if the road widens to a circle for a turnaround.

chapter five

The Resale Home: Your Likely Choice

A resale house is any dwelling that has been lived in by another owner, even if that owner is moving out after only six months in a brand-new home. The resale house is more affordable, generally speaking, than a brand-new one, and can carry a price tag competitive with condos, allowing you to buy a full house rather than an apartment.

Location is not the only factor that determines both satisfaction and investment appreciation. Features should be considered. Features can include architectural details, a floor plan, a window style, a kitchen plan, a basement, a garage, bathrooms, and so forth. Some features add to the enjoyment of the home, others add to its resale value, and some add to both. Then there are features that are negative qualities to some buyers and positive to others.

Your Wish List

Before you get into specific house styles from which to choose, consider what you want in a home. Would you like an eat-in kitchen? How about a room on the first floor that can become your office? Is a garage on your list of must-haves? You may not come up with the house that fills all your needs this time out, but you certainly should be able to meet a few of them.

Features to Look For— and Watch Out For

To buy wisely, you must know what to look for. If you plan to stay in that home for 20 or so years, then you are likely to consider comfort paramount. Most of those who buy intending to move within five to seven years choose investment potential.

Once you establish your priorities, the next step is to recognize which features will add resale value and which will detract from it, as well as which features will add to your living comfort and which will cause inconvenience. This is more of a guessing game than an exact science, so it is impossible to give you an exact list of good and bad features. Every buyer and every selling situation is unique. But it is possible to give you a general idea of the most common home-buyer and homeowner responses to the most wanted and unwanted features. Let's look at some of the features, starting outside and then moving indoors.

View and Landscaping

If you should fall in love with a house with a view, try to buy it without paying for the view. Make your first offer at a price slightly below the market value for a similar house without a view. If the sellers hold firm on their price, however, you will then have to decide exactly how much that view is worth to you.

Siting

Which way is east? North? The answers will affect your heating bill and maybe even your disposition. Which rooms will have morning light? Which will bask in the afternoon sun? Are there rooms that will remain dark most of the day?

Style

Usually, style will positively affect investment potential if it harmonizes with the area and negatively affect it if it jars the eye. If resale value and speed are unimportant to you, you can feel free to choose the unusual or offbeat. If investment appreciation and resale are essential to your purchase, stick with the prevailing styles in that area.

Construction Materials

Brick houses are considered desirable across the country. Wood is also acceptable everywhere, although it is somewhat less desirable in areas where termites are abundant. Vinyl or aluminum siding over a wood frame may or may not add to resale value but will probably save you maintenance time and money.

Stucco is an attractive and widely used material throughout the South, with good buyer acceptance. In the North, however, stucco houses can be hard to sell because their unjointed surfaces are subject to cracking from the changeable weather. Stone and granite facades, on the other hand, have expansion space and rarely cause problems. They are usually attractive, too, which is a selling plus.

Driveways

Blacktop or concrete driveways are most preferred and add to resale speed and value and to owner convenience. Crushed bluestone is acceptable, especially in tract developments where blacktopping the driveway is not included in the price of the house. Gravel driveways, however, are usually a resale and convenience minus.

The large turnaround area of a circular driveway certainly adds to owner convenience, not to mention safety, but rarely affects selling price. A particularly long or steep driveway may not significantly affect resale value but will usually increase the length of time needed to sell the property.

Garages

The attached two-car garage is preferred. Usually, a garage located to the side of a house brings the best buyer response. If it is eight or 10 feet wider than the size needed for two cars, that space can be used for the lawn mower, garden equipment, bicycles, and other gear.

Garages located under the house are less desirable. Many owners complain about drafts in the rooms above and about higher heating and cooling costs. And many object to the fact that getting into the house means climbing a flight of stairs.

Detached garages are unpopular in the North because no one wants to shovel through a foot of snow to get to the car. Carports do not offer a penny extra in offering price. In the South, however, carports are acceptable for the family car, and detached garages are just fine.

Decks, Patios, and Porches

Any place to sit or eat outdoors, while still in the house (relatively speaking), is almost always a plus for both comfort and resale.

Pool

Its value depends on the climate where you're house hunting. Many buyers in the North do not want the work involved in maintaining an above-ground pool that can only be used a few weeks a year. However, in the South a pool is a plus. In both regions buyers with small children might be concerned about a pool.

Windows

Self-insulating windows and sliding glass doors are often considered such positive features that they are specifically mentioned by brand name in advertisements. In the North, houses with neither self-insulating windows nor storm windows lose points. In the deep South, though, screen windows without storms are acceptable. Southern oceanfront properties often feature hurricane shutters to protect both the window glass and the interior of the house or apartment. They are a plus for buyers but do not raise the property's value.

Entranceways

After the first few weeks in a house, the new owners almost always begin using the back door almost exclusively. Still, that front entranceway is an important factor in the salability of a house as it is a would-be buyer's first impression.

Back entranceways do not have much effect on salability, but they certainly play an important role in owners' enjoyment and comfort, especially if there are children or pets in the house. The "ideal" back door opens into a mud room, a back hallway, or cubicle where there is space to hang coats, remove wet boots, or wipe dirty paws. In the most well-planned houses, this back hall is adjacent to or combined with the laundry room, which saves carrying the dirty cloths, rugs, and rags.

Back doors that open directly into the kitchen can be bothersome because of the increased traffic and clutter that they generate, but they are preferable to family room back doors, especially if a patio or outside eating area is serviced by the door. Sliding glass doors are popular and will not hurt resale.

Kitchens

Most home buyers have eat-in kitchens on their list of must-haves. In contrast, long, narrow "pullman-style" kitchens are least popular and will often keep a house on the market a long time. Center islands are positives, as are sinks (especially double sinks) under a window. Counter space is important, and plenty of cabinet space is always mentioned in a sales pitch.

Bathrooms

Today's sellers, it seems, must offer at least one bath and a powder room, and two full baths (or two and a half baths) are preferable. Bathrooms with outside windows are far more appealing to buyers than interior baths with vent fans—but better an interior extra bathroom than none at all.

Walk-in shower stalls are preferable to shower-over-tub arrangements, but most people want at least one bathtub in the house. Bathroom vanities are becoming a must in today's new homes. Double sinks are a plus, too, as are full-wall mirrors behind the sink/vanity. Wallpaper is preferred to paint.

Closets

There are never enough of them. Large bedroom closets are a selling point and a better-living feature. A walk-in closet in the master bedroom is on most buyers' must-have lists. But while going through homes, look for these features too:

- A foyer or front hall closet where you can hang guests' coats
- A linen closet (ideally, one closet—perhaps in a hallway—for sheets and blankets and another in the bathroom for towels)
- A broom or utility closet, preferably near the kitchen
- A back door closet or at least some place to hang family coats and store boots and the like

Bedrooms

We would all like large ones; however, such rooms seem to rank on the luxury level when it comes to home construction, and it is rare to find more than one large bedroom per house. If some of the bedrooms are small, at least look for good wall space for furniture arrangement and easy access to a bathroom.

Family Rooms

Today, family rooms are more important than living rooms and sometimes larger. In the South and West, family rooms are being combined with kitchen and eating areas into great rooms that most buyers seem to like. In contrast, basement family rooms are out of style and almost a detriment to a sale. In the North, family room fireplaces are a major plus.

Fireplace

There are no negatives to this feature. Fireplaces are popular with buyers even if they never light a fire, using the hearth simply as a decorative focal point in a room.

Living Rooms

In a house without a family room, the living room should be as large as possible. But in houses with family rooms, most buyers are more concerned with the location of the living room than with its size. They want the living room to be formal and out of the path of day-to-day traffic. Living room fireplaces are fine but rarely bring a penny more in offering price.

Dining Rooms

Some folks want a formal dining room, but others think just an eat-in kitchen is fine. If there is a formal dining room, it should have a direct doorway to the kitchen and another to the foyer or the living room. If it is separated from the kitchen by stairs or a hallway, as is often found in rehabilitated brownstones, for example, some buyers will turn away from the house.

Attics

The old-fashioned attic, with real stairs, is certainly the most useful kind of home storage space. Such a space often comes only with an older home. Today's modern attics are far less accessible. Pull-down stairs in a hallway are acceptable to most buyers and do provide a means of getting to the holiday decorations each year. Less appealing to buyers and downright inconvenient to homeowners is attic access through a trap door in the ceiling of a bedroom closet.

Basements

Where they are commonly found (primarily in the North), basements are high on a buyer's demand list and high on the homeowner's convenience list. Above all, they should be dry; good lighting is an added plus. Also very desirable is a direct exit from the basement to the outdoors.

In poking around basements, you'll want to know about heat. You can't always get gas heat, which might be your first choice, for low maintenance. Oil heat requires periodic delivery to your home. Electric is the most expensive heating style, although it, too, is low maintenance. Beware of heat pumps in the North, which don't seem to provide quite enough warmth for residents in that part of the country. Heat pumps are fine in the South, though.

When it comes to radiators versus forced air, the disadvantage of radiators or baseboard heat is that you'll need a separate system if you want central air conditioning one day. However, heat is more moist with circulating hot water, which is better for those with allergies. With forced air you can use the same duct for heat and air conditioning, and you'll have either quickly—

within five minutes of flipping a switch. Radiators take longer to heat up a room.

Laundry Facilities

A washer and dryer hookup in the basement is better than no facilities at all, but it will not help a resale. And you, the owner, will not enjoy carrying the laundry up and down the cellar stairs. The most requested laundry facility is a separate room near the kitchen. If that area is large enough to accommodate an ironing board or a sewing machine, it becomes a major selling point for the house. Laundry facilities in the kitchen behind sliding or folding doors do not seem to hurt resale value.

Floor Plans and Traffic Patterns

If you have looked at brand-new homes, you have probably seen floor plans. However, if you are considering an older home, a floor plan will not be available. Mentally walk your way through any older house that interests you. Imagine your daily routine and a special situation such as a party. Where will you come in from work? Where will you hang your coat? Where can you read quietly while the kids are playing video games?

Are there rooms that must be walked through in order to reach other rooms? Only the kitchen is an acceptable walk-through room, and it is often located at or near the activity center of the house. All other walk-through rooms are a detriment to a sale.

What is the traffic pattern between the family living area (the kitchen or family room) and the most often used bathroom? Some lavatories are located off the foyer, which is convenient for guests but inappropriate for the family, especially when muddy children are told to wash up and must walk through the dining room to the lavatory.

The Very Old, Even Historic House

Perhaps the resale home that interests you is not a three-year-old preowned ranch but a 110-year-old Victorian or a 126-year-old farmhouse—in other words, not just an older house but an old house. Or perhaps the only housing stock in the town you like dates to the 1930s.

Do these homes intrigue you? If so, there are some important points to consider. For example, don't let your love for old houses lead you to buy a withering but charming wreck of a structure far beyond your financial capabilities for "fixing it up." Mortgage payments, real-estate taxes, fuel bills, plus a hefty home-improvement loan could be far too much debt for you to handle, especially if you are a first-time buyer and homeowning is new to you.

Be very sure you know if the house that interests you has any historic designation—local, state, or federal. That can well affect how much, or how little, hacking away you will be able to do with repairs or installations. Designation affects how you can treat the outside of the house—setback, paint colors, surface materials, and so forth. Inside, you are on your own, although an addition or bumping out a wall to create a bay window will have to be approved by the state or regional historic district commission.

chapter six

Other Housing Options: Two-Family Houses, Condos, Lofts, and the Fixer-Upper

Could You Become a Landlord?

One of the very best ways to ease yourself into a home of your own and the beginning of what could be a profitable investment career is by purchasing a house that has rental space. Moreover, mortgage lenders often take that rent into account when calculating your mortgage worthiness.

The rent can also pay a good deal of your housing expenses—perhaps your entire mortgage payment or more. This can be a particular relief for those in precarious professions—some of the self-employed, for instance, and those whose positions are always in danger of cutbacks or otherwise subject to the vagaries of the marketplace.

There are other benefits. The repairs and new installations you make to that rental apartment are deductible from your federal tax returns. The apartment's share of your repairs to the house as a whole—a new roof, for example—are also deductible.

Most real-estate investors start with small rental properties. You could find yourself launched on a very profitable sideline or a full-time career as a landlord of several houses or even small apartment buildings.

The Flip Side

On the other hand, here are some points to give you pause with this type of purchase. There will be people—strangers— walking around above or below you. However, if you have lived in an apartment building before, that should not bother you. Others may find it disquieting, for a while. For some, it becomes an everyday part of life.

Private homes converted to two or three separate living units, the type of purchase you would be seeking, do not usually appreciate as quickly in market value as single-family houses. They can also take somewhat longer to sell when you are ready to move.

What Being a Landlord Entails

Can you—should you—become a landlord? You will have to be as responsible owning a two-family house as those landlords who run large apartment complexes are supposed to be. If something is broken, you must fix it—and promptly. You may be able to put up with a roof that leaks, because money is too tight for a roofer right now. But if the tenants are on the top floor, you will have to come up with the cash for repairs immediately. This is not just an ethical point. Tenants are entitled by law to premises that are habitable; any serious lack of repairs that leaves those renters without heat, light, or water, or with rain leaking in through a damaged roof can result in a call to the local landlord/tenant enforcement agency and/or withholding rent.

Smaller repairs are a different story. You do not have to drop everything to fix what is not basic to the apartment and does not contribute to making it fit for habitation. You can add some repairs—an outlet that does not work anymore, for example—to your list and get around to them within a reasonable length of time.

If rent control is in force where you live, you will have to adhere to those regulations. They are set by law, including how often you can raise the rent and by how much.

If you are interested in being a landlord and decide to buy a two- or three-family house, you are entitled to ask for at least one unit (that is likely to be where the owner is living) delivered to you vacant. Have that point included in the sales contract. Your local housing agency may say that a tenant with a lease is entitled to stay until his or her lease runs out. If there are no leases, you can ask that the whole house be delivered vacant. Of course, then you must find new tenants. Much of this can be subject to local regulations.

Finding the Right House

Finding the right house is extremely important because your ability to rent the apartment in your house will depend on several factors. Is the house convenient to the downtown or a suburban office park? Or to a college or university? How about parking? Will the house need excessive repairs? Also make sure to check the rental market in the area. If rentals are readily available, maybe due to many large apartment complexes, you will be competing with modern, efficiently run businesses.

Ask yourself who your tenants are likely to be. If you are in a college town are you willing to rent to students? It may be your only choice. Read real-estate articles in the local paper, not just the advertisements. Above all, find out what the market is like, and what the demographics of the community are.

The Tenant Search

Once you have closed on your property, you probably will waste no time in fixing up the apartment and looking for a tenant. In fact, most home buyers in your situation work on the tenant's unit before their own to get that rental money coming in as quickly as possible.

How do you calculate the amount of rent to charge? Check classifieds, but remember the variables. How nice the apartment is matters, but where the apartment is matters even more. Public transportation, shopping conveniences, and nearby schools can all play a dramatic role in what your rental can fetch. Talk to some local real-estate agents about rents. Some offices will have listings up in their windows (these will usually be the "bargains"), with pictures and prices. Most good services will be helpful. They will want to secure your rental unit as their listing and, in the future, your house when you decide to sell.

Rental agencies usually do not charge a fee to find a tenant. Finder's fees are generally paid by the tenant. Be sure to check the realtor's references. Also, make sure to have the final say in any rental decisions. Screening tenants will probably not be the most enjoyable aspect of being a landlord, but it is of major consequence. Make sure to check references on your own.

You are looking for a tenant who can afford your rent and whose current landlord has no gripes. Be wary of references, however. Some landlords will say anything just to get you to take a poor tenant off their hands. Others fear legal reprisals from saying anything negative. General references are even more useless. The potential tenant's mom and best friend are not going to say anything bad about them.

At the very least, verify the tenants employment and check their credit report. You will need the prospect's permission to access their credit report, but you should feel entitled to insist. In some cases, such as a student, it is common practice to ask for a cosigner to the lease.

Not allowing pets could be a hasty decision you might regret. Because many apartment complexes and housing units ban them, you will be able to find a larger pool of eager, pet-loving applicants. This could allow for a slightly higher rent. Try to secure a pet deposit of $200 or so to cover any cleaning you might have to do after the tenant leaves.

Make sure to have a written lease. A rental agency can take care of this or you can find a standard apartment lease in a stationery or office supply store. Feel free to have special clauses, and make them specific. For example, you might add, "Landlord permits this tenant to bring in his two cats, Bitsy and Axle." That works better than just "pets allowed," which means your tenants could gradually set up their own petting zoo.

Condos

Are you thinking about shopping for a condo? You could save $10,000 to $30,000 or more with a condo apartment over the price of a single-family house, perhaps comprising the same or nearly the same amount of space. You can also frequently enjoy a swimming pool, tennis courts, fitness center, and clubhouse right on the grounds of your complex.

If you are a first-time buyer, you will probably be able to live in a better location with a condo than you would if you purchased a traditional single-family house. That is because you share the expenses of the landscaping and other amenities with the entire condo community. You also share the high property taxes! The condo can also be a reasonably sound investment, allowing a unit owner to trade up to a house, if he or she chooses, or perhaps to a fancier condo complex.

How a Condo Works

Condos date back to ancient Rome and have been in existence in Europe far longer than they have in this country. It is the legal system of ownership that determines a condo, not a building style. Indeed, a condo community can be a high-rise tower in town or a sprawling garden complex in the suburbs. It can be a single-family home community at a lakefront resort, too.

A condominium complex, however it is laid out, is a shared-ownership community. Residents own their own apartment or "unit," or rather they own what is within the exterior walls but not what is outside those walls. They also own a proportional share of what is known as the common areas. Those areas include the apartments' outside walls, driveways and roads inside the complex, garages or carports, and all of the land (including pool or tennis court) within the complex's boundaries, including the landscaping around each unit.

Buying

A condo is purchased the same way as a house. You can work with a realty agent, or you can drive around the community you like, looking for a sign on the lawn advertising a unit for sale by its owner. You apply for a mortgage the same way you do for a new or resale house.

Your mortgage interest is tax deductible, and so are the real-estate taxes for your unit. You are also allowed a tax deduction for your share of real-estate taxes on the common areas. A statement sent to you by the owners' association will inform you of the amount. The monthly maintenance fee is not tax deductible.

Bylaws, Covenants, and Rules and Regulations

Each condo association has its own rulings governing virtually every aspect of life within the community but outside your own four walls. All of these dos and don'ts are designed to keep up the appearance of the development and, by extension, property values.

Read everything, or have your lawyer read all the material you are handed, and ask him or her to check special points that will be of concern to you. For example, the number and size of your pets could be restricted. If you work at home, you might have a problem, unless it is a business that does not depend on people (and their cars) coming to your home (or at least not more than one at a time). Condo residents hate numbers of people coming in with cars and taking their parking spaces.

What Happens If Something Breaks?

This can be one of the major adjustments for those who come from apartment life. If you are used to calling the building super-intendent when there is a problem in your apartment, you will have to adjust to the fact that while you might be living in what looks like an apartment, there is no super. There is no building manager or managing agent you can call when a faucet drips. It is your responsibility to have it repaired or not, just as it is your problem in a single-family house.

All of this is a tricky area, however, which is why your community's bylaws are likely to be such a hefty packet. Take, for example, a burst pipe. It is the responsibility of the association to repair a malfunction if it is caused by a problem in the main or branch pipes serving your apartment. As stated previously, what occurs within your own four walls—for example, a leaky faucet—is for you to repair. However, if you notified the association of a plumbing problem within the common walls, and they failed to repair it before a pipe burst and ruined your carpeting, the association is then likely to be responsible for the damage.

You must also allow access to your apartment in order to get that leak fixed. If you refuse, you could be responsible for the cost of repairs to all of the apartments involved! And if the workers must break through a wall in your unit to get to some defective pipes that are staining someone else's walls, you must allow them access. After the plumber leaves, the association is required to repair your walls and leave the area clean. Whether they or you get to redecorate (paint, wallpaper) is debatable.

Your responsibilities are not exactly those of a tenant or of a totally free owner, either. You are all mutually dependent on one another. You cannot simply call someone and have a repair taken care of (unless you are calling your plumber, electrician, etc.). On the other hand, you do not have to shovel your way from the front door to the street and beyond with each snow-fall—or mow the grass and trim the hedges around your unit—or paint its exterior.

Beware of Overbuilding!

While condo buying can be quite successful, it can be almost disastrous in some situations. The huge amount of overbuilding of condo complexes in some parts of the country, and in some parts of any town or city, for that matter, has brought a glut of units to the market. You have to be very careful not to buy in a saturated neighborhood, where it may be difficult to sell or you'll have to sell for less than your purchase price because of a proliferation of other apartments for sale.

Selecting the Right Condo

Most condo complexes do look, well, nice. Is that enough? Unfortunately, no. You may notice that in some communities, maintenance could be better. There is nothing outrageously wrong, but the trim around the exterior doors and windows needs a coat of paint. Or some of the mortar between the outside bricks is crumbling. Does that mean the association is lax about mainte-nance? It could be, although it is more likely that there are no funds for repairs!

Reading the Financial Statement

Major repairs and improvements in a condo must be paid for by special assessments to the unit owners. It is important that a healthy condo community have a contingency fund for emergency expenses and a reserve for future improvements or repairs. A portion of each unit owner's maintenance fee should be put into those funds.

Read through the financial statement to see if there have been any recent special assessments. Ask members of the board and the management company, if there is one, if any major changes or repairs are being contemplated.

Lofts

A house is not just a home to *you*. *You* want to live in a trendy neighborhood as a resident of . . . a hat factory? Well, at one time it was a hat factory. Right now it is perhaps another example of a strong back-to-the-city movement in one urban section of your metropolitan area.

Or maybe the loft is in a former factory or any other industrial building where the company died or moved to newer facilities, leaving behind a vacant structure. Over the last two decades, those handsome buildings, usually found downtown and/or along a community waterfront, have been rescued from abandonment to become attractive and—in the beginning, anyway—affordable housing.

Lofts can offer many pluses to the house hunter of any age:

- You'll be living in a home with a history, sometimes of a century or more.
- It's affordable housing, at least in some cities where housing is not sky high and the loft movement is still new. In downtown Denver, for example, one- and two-bedroom lofts in a

former department store are priced from the $70s to the low $100s. They are handsomely appointed and boast a furnished atrium lobby on each of its floors, a community meeting room, exercise facility, TV and billiard lounges, and an enclosed parking garage available to loft owners only.

- Lofts often feature abundant living space.
- Even though it may be a converted factory, there is almost always ample natural light. Many lofts boast huge floor-to-ceiling—and high ceilings at that—windows with marvelous downtown views.
- You'll enjoy city life, most likely being very close to the downtown area.
- Fellow building residents, because of their housing choice and preference, often become more than just neighbors.
- Since the buyer may be the first, or no more than the second or third, owner of that home, appliances, flooring, ceramic tile, and other features are practically brand new.

Is there a downside to all this enthusiasm?

- Lofts can be quite pricey. In New York's SoHo, the district in Manhattan where the loft movement began in that city, the artists who originally settled there before the area took off in the 1970s have given way to high-income residents living in lofts costing well into six (and more often seven) figures. Affluent buyers now dominate the loft market.
- Some lofts that are affordable may be raw space. Meaning after you buy it you must pay to install electricity, plumbing, walls, appliances, fixtures, and so on. This gets very expensive and is a lot of work.
- In manufacturing areas, loft residents might have quite a trek just to get to the grocery store.

- Some loft buildings are not up to local regulations and codes. The building could be forced to building and safety code compliance, at the expense of loft dwellers. There may not be adequate rear yards, for example, to meet a city's fire, safety, and air requirements. The solution? In that instance, it could be necessary to remove parts of the building.

Ah, but the positives of this living experience far outweigh the few negatives, right? So, how do you buy a loft?

Your best bet is to hang around, literally, the loft area that interests you. Talk to residents. Read real-estate ads. See what the prices are and what is going on in that neighborhood. What are residents angry about? What are they doing about it? How is city hall treating loft dwellers? Gather as much information as you can before stopping in at a realty office to loft shop.

Buying a Fixer-Upper

The most important points to consider when buying a fixer-upper are 1) know how much repair work you can actually take on and complete once the initial wave of rehabbing enthusiasm passes, and 2) avoid houses in which major repairs are needed. In other words, stay away from houses with serious defects in the foundation or working systems (such as heating, electrical, or plumbing) or in which a major reshuffling of rooms is necessary to create a workable traffic pattern. All of this work is expensive, and you may not see much of your financial investment returned when you sell. A buyer will expect workable plumbing and heating, adequate wiring, and so on. A new roof comes under the heading of a major improvement, though this can add to value because it improves the appearance of the home.

Neophytes should stick to houses that need painting, landscaping, minor to medium-size repairs, carpeting, and other cosmetic improvements. Upgrading the kitchen and bathroom(s) can also be profitable when it comes to resale, and so will adding a second bathroom.

Use your own judgment in determining how much fixing up you can undertake, both emotionally and financially. There are a number of points to keep in mind while shopping for the least expensive yet potentially most salvageable and profitable fixer-upper.

Prices for shabby properties might be almost as high as prices for houses in better condition. It is important not to overpay for any house but particularly important not to spend all of your money on a house that needs still more money—and big bucks at that—to make it look good.

If the fixer-upper you are considering has been on the market for a long time, ask yourself why. Location aside, it might be that it needs a lot of work, but it could be other reasons. Let's say the house is very dark and dreary inside. That defect could be remedied by installing a skylight or two, an idea that might not have occurred to other house shoppers. Be creative as you go through these homes. Knowing how to fix flaws that might put off other buyers to a basically sound property could bring you an excellent deal.

As you walk through fixer-uppers, make notes on repairs needed (a house inspector will do a more thorough job later). Then take out your calculator when you return home and figure roughly how much you will need in upgrading costs. If you cannot estimate the costs to remedy some malfunction or other, at least list the problem, with a repair figure to be filled in later. Seeing a sizable list of wrongs could well change your mind about buying a particular property.

Speaking of work, consider who will do the repairs in the house you buy. It is most cost effective if the owners do most of the work themselves, with a little guidance from the local home decorating center. The pros are called on only for highly specialized areas such as electrical work, heating, some plumbing, and the like.

Look into local zoning restrictions. Be sure that you can renovate the way you want, particularly if you want to add an extension to the house. Perhaps you will not be permitted to do so, or perhaps you will require a variance. Are you sure you can win one? Do you want to go to that trouble?

Is the renovation work going to be so drastic, or so messy, that you will be unable to live in the house until most of the work is complete? If so, where will you live? Can you afford to carry a mortgage payment and rent where you are now, perhaps along with a home repair loan payment each month?

If you feel you can—or must—live there while work is in progress, try to organize your space to settle in for the long haul. Be certain your family, and your marriage, can stand the strain of the always-present odor of sawdust and paint, the constant walking around ladders and planks of wood.

A house inspection makes good sense in buying any resale home. It is vital to know what you're getting into before putting down your life savings on a house that could be a problematic investment.

What Should You Pay for a Fixer-Upper?

When considering what to offer, take the market value of the house, deduct what you think repairs will cost, add a little extra in the event you lowballed the repairs figure, and you should come up with a fair offer. Another formula: How much would this house be worth if it were in top-grade condition? Consider that the asking price is $95,000, but, with some improvements, it could one day bring $115,000. You should buy at 20 to 30 percent below what the house would cost if it were not a fixer-upper.

In the sales contract, include this phrase: "subject to the buyer obtaining a satisfactory inspection report and satisfactory repair bids within 10 business days." The inspection is standard these days; the repair bids phrase should be incorporated in fixer-upper bids. If you do not approve of the reports and recommendations you receive from the house inspector and from the repair people you call in for estimates, you can cancel the agreement to purchase and have your earnest money deposit refunded.

If a fixer-upper needs a good deal of work, many buyers skip calling in a house inspector and instead call a contractor—the person they will engage later to do the repair work—to look at the property. Naturally, they stick close to that individual as he goes through the property, jotting down his comments to familiarize themselves with, and make sure they remember, the house's problems.

Home-Improvement Loans

If the home you buy needs repairs or improvements, you will have to come up with some money for that renovation. Or perhaps it's in fair shape, but you'd like another bathroom. In any event, you may need some more money to make your home into what you envision.

Besides the tried-and-true lender sources already covered, there are loan sources not that familiar to many of us. These sources sometimes offer good borrowing terms, especially if they are federal or state government programs.

The 203(k) program, offered by the federal government through the FHA, enables the buyer of a one- to four-family house to borrow both the sale price for the house and its renovation loan. The loan amount offered is based on the estimated after-refurbishing value of the house.

The maximum amount you can borrow is subject to FHA lending guidelines for that particular geographic area (there are no income caps for buyers, however). The minimum you can borrow is $5,000. Financing is based on an estimate of the value of the home after renovations, with the mortgage and renovation loan created for that total amount. Interest rates are slightly higher than conventional mortgage rates but lower than rates for conventional renovation loans.

Another popular federal-government loan source is the FHA Title 1 program, in which the FHA insures loans made by private lenders for as much as $25,000. The payback period can be as long as 20 years. Interest charged might be higher than with a home equity loan but lower than a home-improvement loan from a commercial lender. The interest is tax deductible.

Check with Fannie Mae, too. That agency has renovation mortgages for people who will live in their fixed-up houses. Fannie Mae's HomeStyle program permits buyers to purchase and fix up more expensive houses than those allowed by the 203(k) program. Interest rates can be better, too. The loan limit is $214,000.

chapter seven

A House Built Just for You

Perhaps you consider building a home to be a money-saving venture. Or maybe you just want a sparkling, brand-new house, and cost is not a major concern for you. Whatever your reason, you will need a bit of the good earth on which to construct your dream.

If you go land shopping, 1) keep in mind that costs for vacant acreage have been rising steadily, and 2) do not be so eager to buy and build that you make a serious error with the lot you select. You can probably pay $2,000 for a one-acre lot somewhere, but it might be impossible to build a home on that site. It may not be accessible to utilities. It may be so far off the beaten track that it is difficult to reach. It could have poor drainage. Maybe it is not zoned for a home.

Shopping for a Site

Be sure to look at environmental concerns. It will pay to check into what your state environmental agency has, or has in mind, for land trust purposes and where it could be putting a total moratorium on development.

Don't buy too close to a major highway. You might find that your state highway department is planning to widen a road right into your parlor. Check as many master plans and environmental agency reports as you can for the area you are considering.

Find out if the land can be used as a home site. What type of permit must be obtained? Are there water and sewer hookups? Is your lot large enough, according to local zoning laws, for the construction of a home? All of this can be checked at your city or town hall.

More than a few buyers have been dismayed to learn that the lot they purchased is too small, according to local government restrictions, for the house they want to build—or for any house. Make sure the lot you buy is large enough for the home you have in mind. Check also that the lot is not too steep for building, another unpleasant surprise for some buyers.

Also check the soil. You might have to add topsoil to your lot or take some topsoil away from it. Rock that is too close to the soil can add to the expense of the foundation or make digging one totally impractical. A high water table or a ground not stable enough to support a house could run into still more expense. Be especially wary of acreage over a landfill, where flooding can occur as the water table rises. Ask about all of this at your town engineer's office.

Find out if you can erect a manufactured home—your most affordable choice—on the lot. There are some municipalities with regulations against such houses.

Utilities are another point to check. Is the lot you are looking at serviced by public sewer and water? If not, you will need a septic system and a well.

Will you be landlocked? The selling of landlocked lots is illegal in many states. Small plots in the middle of nowhere that can be reached only by helicopter cannot be marketed anymore. There must be an access road.

What will be going up around you? Again, look at local master plans to see what kind of growth is forecast. Ask around, too, to see what is in the talking stages for the acreage around the lot you have selected.

What about the shape of that lot? The more road frontage on an already completed thoroughfare, the more valuable the piece of land will be. The more expense required to develop the land, the cheaper your purchase price should be.

Do not forget resale value. Being plunked in the woods far from even the nearest hamlet might suit you fine. But when it comes time to sell, buyers with a similar preference might be fewer than you would like.

Finally, you cannot forget the local political entity where you buy. Learn to whom you report building plans, requests, problems, and the like. If you have to appear before a zoning board or a city council meeting to petition for a zoning variance, try to get a reading on those people. How do they feel about development, even on the small scale you are planning? Are you likely to win your variance?

The Very Affordable Manufactured or Modular Home

Manufactured or modular homes are produced in sections—that can include even carpeting—and then shipped to the building site where the parts are assembled to form a house. Some are very plush and virtually indistinguishable from site-built (in the ground) homes.

Home buyers (and developers) choose these homes for one simple reason: They are usually less costly than site-built homes of similar size. An average three-bedroom, two-bath house, with amenities, can cost under $50,000, including setup or installation (but excluding the cost of land). Larger homes can carry $100,000-plus price tags.

If you own land and want to have a manufactured or modular home put on your lot, you can contact one of the more than one hundred companies nationwide that build these houses. They are represented by thousands of retailers around the country. The company you call can put you in touch with the retailer nearest you. Some manufacturers have their own sales centers in certain parts of the country, too, where you can also buy.

If a manufactured or modular home is permanently set on a foundation and is sold with land or erected on land owned by the new homeowner, it usually can be financed with a real-estate mortgage from the same variety of lenders that offer financing for site-built homes. The key here is that the home and land are considered a single real-estate entity under state law.

Manufactured homes on rented land and houses that are considered personal property rather than real estate (the old style mobile homes come under this definition) are treated differently and are not financed as real estate with a mortgage. Manufactured home retailers can arrange financing for these purchases, or you can shop around for better terms at banks and other lending institutions in your area.

How about a New Development Home?

New houses are, as you might expect, more expensive than resale homes, all things being equal. Still, with a new home you can have all the space you need. It can be as light and bright as you want. New means cutting-edge technologies, too.

You might want to consider purchasing a new house in a development. With some canny shopping, you might even be able to strike a price deal for yourself.

How to Find These New Affordables

You can start by looking beyond the city limits and most likely beyond the suburbs. You will get a better deal on homes way, way out, where the developer has not paid astronomical rates for land. Where such homes are situated is vitally important. Part of the attraction of such developments is their price. But you will probably want a reasonable number of existing services there now.

Another suggestion for finding affordables: Look for the innovative builders in your area who specialize in quality medium-cost construction. A call to your statewide builders association can bring you their names, as well as some addresses for you to check out.

When looking at new construction, beware—just as you would in a traditional neighborhood—of the largest, flashiest house in a development. Look instead at the mid-priced or lower-end models. The value of those homes will be pulled up by the splashier ones around them. The only exception would be a community that stresses recreational amenities, where being right on the golf course, say, or on the lake would be the top-of-the-line location that buyers would be willing to spend money to acquire.

Negotiating to Sweeten the Deal

Developers do not usually like to lower sales prices of their homes. However, the state of the economy (both national and local), the developer's finances, and other factors could make him quite amenable to "talking." The trick here is to keep cool. As with other types of negotiating, it is not a good idea to seem too excited about what someone is trying to sell you.

When a community is essentially finished and running smoothly, a developer may well want to "close out" that complex as quickly as possible. If there are two or three houses that remain stubbornly unsold, a developer might lower their prices. Occasionally, the model home might be sold that way, although it could also be sold early, with the deal not formally enacted until the developer is prepared to close down sales. The developer who has many unsold homes is also likely to be amenable to some negotiating. In the off season for home buying—generally October through January or February—when developers are drumming their fingers on desktops in sales offices, you will also look very welcome, and all of the stops might be pulled out to keep you from looking elsewhere.

More likely than a price cut is negotiation over what will be included in a sales price, which will stay firm. All the little extras can add up, and it is up to you to ask for them. Perhaps a house is selling for $125,000, and you know you are going to spend another, say, $6,000 for decorating features you want. If you get $3,000 from the developer in the form of extras, that is $3,000 you won't have to spend.

Be careful, though, with frills. If the builder says, "I'll cut the price by $5,000 or give you $5,000 in credit that youcan use to buy the things you want from our design center," take the price cut. There is usually quite a markup on developers' upgrades.

Buying a House Before It Is Built

Buying a home before it is built carries its own potential price savings. In the real-estate section of your local paper, you will often see advertisements offering preconstruction prices. A pre-construction price is the first price at which a new development home is offered. That is when, say, Sherwood Glen is probably still a sea of mud and a sales trailer. Developers concede they underprice a little at the beginning to get the ball rolling. Nothing brings in customers more than seeing other people buy.

How much can you save at this stage? Houses sold when the development is complete can cost 20 to 30 percent more than the price of preconstruction homes! Buying early also gives you a choice of location. However, one problem might be some uncertainty about when you will actually have the house. Sometimes there are construction delays and delivery snags. If you need to get into your new home right away, you could become a nervous wreck.

It is important that you know your builder. It is best to go with someone who has done similar construction and has completed such jobs. Look for a builder with a record of other single-family home projects. Drive around his or her other projects, even if you have to head 30 miles out of town. Talk to those homeowners if you can, too, and ask them if they are satisfied with their houses.

If you are one of the early residents in a development, will you feel comfortable living virtually alone until more people move in? What about the safety factor? Can children play in the area without the danger of their running into construction materials or, worse, machinery? Will you mind the noise of construction? Just how primitive will life be as a pioneer settler?

Once a contract is signed, the sales figure—preconstruction or not—is usually protected no matter how many times a developer later raises the cost of those homes. If you are concerned about a delivery delay, ask for a clause in the contract requiring the builder to notify you two months in advance of the completion date; thus, you will establish a time frame for changing residence.

Checking Out the Place Before You Move In

You might be allowed one inspection of your home after it is framed up (so that you can see what is going up behind the walls) and then another inspection after the drywall is installed (to avert any problems during the final inspection). Last comes your final walk through (to be followed by one by your lender). At the last look at the house before closing, you have the opportunity to assure yourself that the builder has completed the job to your satisfaction.

Anything that has not been completed or is not up to standard should be jotted down on what is known as a punch list, a sheet prepared for buyers for just that reason. Do not be so taken with how marvelous the house looks that you do not check every detail. This is your chance to have things set to rights. Ask the builder to fix the points ticked off on your punch list before the closing. Then make a final inspection to see that indeed those problems have been corrected.

Sometimes a builder will contest your complaint. If a problem remains unsolved as closing nears, you can delay the closing until all of the questionable points have been cleared up. If the builder offers you cash instead of repairs, decline and ask for the repairs. They could cost more than the builder's cash allowance.

Remember that you hold all the cards before the closing. If ever there is a time to get the corrections you want, this is it. Your leverage drops way down after you take title to the house.

The Custom-Built Home

If you know exactly the type of house you want but can't seem to find the development home that fits, then you should consider a custom-built home. Building your own home can be a creative, exhilarating experience. It also can be a frustrating, time- and money-consuming one, too.

Working with an Architect or a Custom Builder

How can you get your custom-designed house built as smoothly—and economically—as possible? First, know where you are going to place that special home. If you have good land, with access to water and sewer facilities and on a level lot in a community where you can build just what you want, then, literally and figuratively, you have a good foundation for your construction project. And second, choose the right architect or custom builder for you.

An Architect

An architect's fee will increase the cost of your new home by about 10 percent, but you might well make that up in resale value, not to mention your enjoyment of a well-planned house during your years living there. By overseeing your project carefully, an architect might be able to get discounts for you on materials. That alone could eat up that 10 percent.

Talk with some architects in the area where you are looking. They know the land, the weather, and any eccentricities of that area better than one who lives far away.

You will want an architect who shares your vision of a home, whether it's a Victorian, a sleek stone and glass contemporary, or a charming, compact Cape Cod. An architect whose portfolio consists of homes you cannot identify with is obviously not on your wavelength. Keep looking.

Once your building project has begun, you can hire the architect to oversee the work, if you have neither the time nor the familiarity with construction yourself. He or she is likely to charge $100 an hour or so.

The Custom Builder

A custom builder, who does not have to be an architect and indeed is almost never an architect, can also design a home on a computer to your specifications and then construct it.

Once you have chosen an overall design for your house and you have the drawings and specifications, you need to solicit bids from the person who will build that house—the builder (sometimes known as the contractor).

Just as you did with the architect, ask the builder for references and contact those people. Did their home come in on time? On budget or close to it? Have any problems surfaced since they moved in? Did the builder fix them promptly?

Naturally, if you engage a custom builder, he or she will oversee the project as part of the job. Since your builder is also designing your home, the cost for those plans will be included in the overall fee.

New-Home Warranties

You will most likely receive a builder's warranty—usually a one-year protection plan—against problems with your new house. Like most warranties, these plans cover the house against structural defects and malfunctions of the working systems. However, if your builder goes under or is no longer on the scene for some other reason, you will be out of luck; your chances of being reimbursed for repairs will be practically nonexistant.

However, if your house is covered by an insured, independent warranty, you are home clear. Such plans are usually 10-year policies written by an independent warrantor, such as Home Owners Warranty (HOW). If anything goes awry with your builder, your claim—if considered a legitimate one—will be honored by those warrantors.

Try to secure both a builder's and an independent warranty. Of course, as already stated, you will most likely have the builder's one-year protection. You can use his or her payment of the insured policy premium as a negotiating tool. In the event he or she firmly refuses to offer a warranty, you should purchase a policy on your own. A few hundred dollars is little to pay to insure the proper functioning of an investment of many times that figure.

chapter eight

House Hunting with a Real-Estate Agent—and on Your Own

Now that you know how much house you can afford and what you need and prefer in a home, you are ready for serious home shopping.

How a Realty Agent Can Help

Take advantage of the many services offered by real-estate agencies. They will cost you nothing because it is usually the seller of the house who pays the agent fee. House hunters, especially first timers, are foolish if they do not use the help of these professionals. A knowledgeable realty agent can direct you to the pool of properties likely to interest you and away from totally unacceptable houses that will only waste your time and energy. An agent can provide you with help in several phases of the buying process.

- *Qualifying for a mortgage.* The real-estate agent might be plugged into a lending institution you did not contact or can steer you to a good financing package.
- *Supplying local information.* Information on property taxes, schools, neighborhoods, recreation facilities, and so on should be on the tip of every agent's tongue. Most agents will offer you a street map of their area, which will be invaluable for drive-by tours without the agent and for poking around surrounding regions.
- *Using multiple listing service tools.* Go through the real-estate office's listing sheets on nearly all the property that is for sale in a given community, by price, with pictures, and with all pertinent sales information; your house hunt will be less tiring and a lot more thorough.
- *Offering comparables.* Most real-estate agencies have listings of houses that sold in the previous year, with both their asking and selling price. This should prevent you from overpaying.
- *Evaluating properties.* The agent should get to know your preferences and eliminate undesirable properties without dragging you out to see them.

Understanding the Term "Disclosure"

Disclosure has two distinct uses in a real-estate transaction. First, real-estate agents must disclose to would-be buyers that they represent the seller. Many buyers do not know that extremely important fact about the buying process. The seller pays the agent's commission from proceeds from the sale of the home. Agents' loyalties are with the seller, although they may very well be genuinely helpful to you and sincerely interested in your finding a home you like.

Because of an agent's relationship with the seller you should not disclose exactly how much you will pay for a home. If you have been approved for a mortgage, both you and the agent know your price range. Do not be any more specific than "we want to look at something costing no less than maybe $120,000 and no more than $135,000." Don't give away your bargaining hand by telling the seller the specific dollar that you will spend.

The second use of the word disclosure refers to the agent and seller bringing any problems with the house to the attention of potential buyers, hiding nothing. Disclosure can also apply to a seller's or agent's knowledge of plans for the community or the street on which the house stands that could turn off a prospective buyer.

In any event, you cannot afford to accept passively what agents say—or do not say—and move on to the next buying stage. Poke around on your own to be sure the many questions raised in these chapters are answered to your satisfaction.

Finding the Right Agent

If you are seriously considering several towns in your region, you should probably find a different agent for each—an agent's knowledge of his or her turf is one of the major benefits of the service. You should also find someone with whom you feel comfortable; someone who is knowledgeable and hardworking.

Once you find an agent, stick with him or her. In areas where a multiple listing service is commonly used, your agent can show you any property advertised by any member office. When you see another office's ad in the paper for a property you think you might be interested in, tell your agent and he or she can find out more about it for you. Even when a property is not listed on a multiple listing service, most realty offices are happy to co-broker—that is, allow another agent to show their listing for a split commission if the house hunter buys that property.

How do you find the top-drawer agent? The best method is through personal referral. Ask friends who have recently purchased a home. Another good strategy is reading the large display advertisements in your local paper or the paper for the town where you would like to move; that is where real-estate offices congratulate their top performers. Call one of those stars, and make an appointment for an interview.

Attending open houses may be an activity you are used to by now. Talking with the agent stationed there for the day incurs no obligation on your part and may yield one with whom you can work.

Two of the more chancy methods of finding an agent are calling an office in response to an ad you have seen and walking into an office and saying you want to buy a home. Most realty offices assign their agents floor time. Any prospect who calls in response to advertising or who walks in the door with no appointment is assigned to the agent who has drawn floor time that day. Unfortunately, floor time is not assigned by competence, just by rote. A slight improvement on that poor strategy is asking for the listing agent for the property in the ad you have noted. That will at least direct you to the person who knows all about the home that interests you.

The Buyer's Broker

If you are interested in this concept, there are a couple of points to ponder. First, you should not have to sign a contract with a buyer's broker. But if you must, make it for no longer than 30 or

60 days. A snag could arise when you are looking at homes in towns 15 to 30 miles from one another. Unlike the traditional realty agents, your buyer's broker may represent only one area, meaning you would need another individual for the town 15 miles away.

Second, fees for this service can vary. Sometimes a FSBO seller will pay half a buyer broker's fee. If you are charged $150 or so for a broker's service in finding you the home you buy, make sure you do not pay that sum up front, at the beginning of your house hunt. You should not have to pay anything initially to get a broker to work for you.

A Few Words about Discrimination

It does still exist, of course, despite governmental, professional, and civic efforts. Race is the most obvious basis for discrimination, but religion, national origin, sex, marital status, and children in the family all may predispose an agent to show or not show certain properties to certain people. Such activity is called steering and is against the law.

If you feel you are being steered, for a reason other than your ability to afford the home in question, you can change the situation. Call or write your local Board of Realtors first. You can find that group listed in the white pages of the phone book or in the Yellow Pages where real-estate agents run their advertisements. In the corner of some of the larger ads, there is likely to be a line such as "Member, Upstate County Board of Realtors."

If you are not satisfied with their reaction, contact the National Association of Realtors (NAR) at 430 North Michigan Avenue, Chicago, IL 60611. Their phone number is (312) 329-8200. An investigation will follow.

If you wish to take this action against discriminatory practices further, you can notify your state real-estate commission.

Proven cases of discrimination can result in suspension or loss of license for the agent involved. Sometimes just the threat of reporting discriminatory practices will put an end to them. Another source of advice is your local community housing resources board.

Making the House Hunt Easier

Even if you work with a real-estate agent, you will need some system to your search to keep from short-circuiting after all you have seen and heard. First, be sure the agent knows the type of home you want, the price range, and the architectural style. Specify absolute needs, such as four bedrooms or a two-car garage or being close to the parkway.

Second, limit yourself to viewing no more than six to eight properties in one day. Beyond that number, features blur in your mind and fatigue affects your perceptions. Similarly, give a day to each town, if you are interested in several. By concentrating on separate towns on different days, you will get a good idea of comparative value.

Third, by all means drive around in the agent's car. Chauffeuring is also his or her business. While the agent is driving, you can take notes, mark your street map, or just take in the view. Following the agent in your own car is not a good idea. Being with the agent allows you to ask questions as they occur. You can always talk privately back at home or on the drive home.

No Agents Involved

There are instances in which homes are for sale with no agent involved. These instances include the sale of distressed properties and houses sold at auction.

Distressed Properties

Distressed properties are houses and condominiums in which the owners have defaulted in paying their mortgage, property taxes, or water bills. Foreclosure procedures vary from one community to the next, between federal and local agencies, and between government-backed and private mortgage holders.

In the area of nonpayment of local property taxes and water bills, you can contact your tax collector or other public official who conducts the tax sales and ask about the next auction of those properties. After you see the list and investigate the addresses, contact your lawyer to see if you can purchase the property directly from the owner.

The U.S. Department of Housing and Urban Development (HUD) also sells its foreclosures (houses taken for nonpayment of FHA-backed loans). Those homes and condos are usually sold through sealed bids. That means would-be buyers send in their best offer to the office handling the sale, and the highest bid wins the house or condo. Financing is arranged through a conventional mortgage lender and insured by the FHA. Down-payment requirements can be as low as a few hundred dollars with some incentive programs. Buyers can finance up to 100 percent of the closing costs, including the initial mortgage insurance premium required by the FHA.

Call the number listed on the advertisement in your area newspaper offering HUD homes for sale. Or phone your regional or field HUD office. Or you can call toll free the national HUD Homes Information System at (800) 366-4582; it offers recorded information around the clock.

In addition, you might get in touch with the Department of Veterans Affairs for their list of VA foreclosures. The Federal National Mortgage Corporation (Fannie Mae) has homes for sale acquired through foreclosure. You can call Fannie Mae at (800) 732-6643 during business hours.

In the private sector, houses are also sold by banks that have taken them back for mortgage default. Contact the real-estate-owned (REO) department of any bank, and ask whether they have a list of their foreclosed properties. Some banks deal directly with prospective buyers for those houses; others turn them over to a local real-estate agency to sell for them. Start with the bank first.

If a lender is really eager to get rid of an REO property, it could make the mortgage financing very attractive, with a low (10 percent or sometimes even 5 percent) down-payment requirement and good interest rates. That's what make REO properties worth pursuing—not their sale price, which is usually no great bargain.

Houses Sold at Auction

Some houses, not necessarily distressed properties, are sold through auctions. Sometimes just one home is being sold, perhaps to close an estate. In other instances, the auction will include a number of condominium units in a complex in which the developer has run into financial problems.

Before attending an auction with the serious intent of buying a house or condominium, you should do some homework. Try to acquire all of the printed material on the sale that you can (known as the bidder's kit), and visit the homes that interest you.

There are two golden rules at auctions. One is *caveat emptor*, or let the buyer beware. The second is "as is, where it is." That expression means what it says: There are no refunds, exchanges, or adjustments at the auction. (However, depending on the laws of the state where you are buying, you might have the right to cancel your purchase within an allotted number of days following the sale.) You cannot blame the seller for not telling you the basement floods regularly. Keep this point in mind as you raise your hand or card to bid.

Watch for the announcement of dates when prospective bidders can go through properties being auctioned. Naturally, you should take a detailed look at any home that interests you. You can bring a house inspector or engineer with you, too, to give you an idea of any serious problems and the price for fixing them.

Ask about the title, too. Will you own the house free and clear? Check with the people at the administration desk at the auction, or ask in advance at the auction company or real-estate agency handling the sale.

Ask in advance how the auction handles the actual buying of the homes. Some are strictly cash sales. You will almost certainly be required to pay some small amount of money in order to bid. Be sure you understand whether, if you are a winning bidder, you will be given an allotted time after the auction to secure financing or whether you must be preapproved before the sale.

It will help if the property you want is not one of the opening two or three. That way you can become familiar with the speed of the process before your prospective home comes on the block. Be very sure you are bidding on the property you want. With the speed of the proceedings, mix-ups can occur.

With some auctions of a few dozen properties, an on-site lender can offer good financing terms because that institution expects to finance a good number of homes sold during that sale. Ask about their terms, of course, but shop around to see if you can do better.

chapter nine

Negotiating for the Best Price and the Best Contract

You have to determine the fair price of the home you want before you make an offer for it. This is defined as the highest price a ready, willing, and able buyer will pay and the lowest a ready, willing, and able seller will accept. To be completely accurate, fair market value cannot be established until a property is actually sold. But the trick of an estimate is to come as close to the figure for which you could turn around after the closing and sell the house again quickly (probably in three months or so).

You can make your market evaluation by comparing the property you want to buy with similar properties that have been sold in the area during the past year. You will already have a feel for the price from all the house hunting you have been doing.

What Is "Fair Market Value"?

When you are ready to start negotiating, ask your realty agent to show you comparables. Almost every real-estate office that belongs to a multiple listing organization will have a comparables file or a computerized comparables book. Even independent agencies that do not share listings will keep a file of properties sold by their own offices and agents.

After you have seen comparables, make a list of selling prices and addresses of the properties that you consider similar to "yours." Take home photocopies of those listing sheets, if the agent is willing and allowed to give them to you. Compare and rate each property against "your" house.

When you finish that homework, you will know exactly what other people in the area have had to pay for a certain amount of house in the same or a similar neighborhood. From here, stepping along to an evaluation of what "your" house is worth is relatively easy.

Once you have set what you think is a fair selling price for the property, compare it with what the sellers are asking. If your evaluation price is higher than the asking price (that rarely occurs), do not get out your pen to sign an offer. Look again at the property, the neighborhood, the location, the lot, the time on the market, local conditions—everything. You may have missed something very important. However, if everything checks out, then act quickly. The sellers may just have underpriced their property; so buy before word gets out and another buyer appears and starts a bidding war. However, it is much more likely that the asking price will be more than your estimate of fair market value.

You would be smart to buy a small notebook for this process and make it your negotiating journal. On the first page, record the addresses and prices of your comparables. On the next page, record your ideal price for the home you want (likely to be a "steal" price), your fair market value estimate, and your absolutely "top dollar" price.

Do not tell your real-estate agent your "top dollar figure"— or your "steal" figure either. Remember, the agent represents the seller. You have to play your hand close to the vest during the negotiating process, even with your agent.

The Market at the Moment

Besides checking comparables and working the numbers, it is important that you gauge the state of the market in your area at the time you want to buy. For example, if it is a hot sellers' market, where properties are moving quickly and "your" home is a desirable one with wide potential market appeal, start your negotiations fairly close to market value. You do not want to lose the property playing games over price.

On the other hand, if the market is soft where you are looking (sometimes called a buyers' market) or if the seller is under need-to-sell stress or if the house is not particularly appealing to most people, you can move more slowly and negotiate over a wider range. In these situations, it is possible to get a much better deal with a bit of patience and perseverance.

Your Initial Offer

There is no one "good" initial offer based upon asking price. Why? Because there are so many variables in real estate and because sellers rarely set their asking prices with consideration to market value or other rational thought processes. They are out to get the most they can for their properties, and many have emotional ties to their home that turn Cape Cods into castles. Would you offer 10 percent less than the asking price of a home that is overpriced by $25,000 or more?

Each and every piece of real property is unique, and so is each and every selling situation. But if you must have a guideline, a first offer that is 10 percent below your fair market value estimate—not the seller's asking price—will keep you from insulting the seller. It will also keep you from having your first offer snapped up because it was higher than the seller's what-we-hope-to-get-for-this-place price.

Okay, so you have a figure in mind for your first offer. How do you go about making that offer?

Your offer cannot be verbal. Most residential sales agents will refuse to present a verbal offer that is not accompanied by an earnest money check and specific information on financing, closing date, and other details of the sale. Your offer must be presented to the sellers in writing.

When your real-estate agent hears the word offer, he or she might whip out a binder, a short form that includes your name and address, a few lines about the property being bid on, and the amount of your earnest money deposit (usually $500 or $1,000). If you are handed a binder, be certain it contains the clause "subject to review by the buyer's attorney within five business days." That will allow you to have your lawyer look over the form (and also allow you an out if you change your mind about that property).

However, most agents will want you to sign a contract before they present your offer to the seller. The amount of the earnest money remains the same. If you sign the contract and if the seller likes your offer and also signs that form, you have bought the house.

The Contract

There is really no such thing as a standard purchase contract, although your real-estate agent may say that is what he or she is handing you. There is some information that must be included in every contract, but any contract can include almost anything. The following six items must be included in the contract:

1. *Date*. A contract must be dated to be a legal instrument.
2. *Names*. That means the full names of all of the buyers and all of the sellers.
3. *Price*. The full purchase price should be listed; it is what you are agreeing to.
4. *Address of the property being sold*. A street address is acceptable, unless there are no numbers on the houses—in which case you'll need at least a block and lot number from the local tax map. If you are buying a condo or a co-op, be sure the apartment number and the building number, if necessary, appear in the contract, along with the street address.
5. *Date and place of closing*. This is a date that is frequently changed, but having a named place and time to transfer the property is an essential part of an agreement to purchase.
6. *Signatures*. Each person who rightfully owns and is selling the property and each person buying that property must sign the contractual agreement.

Other Considerations and Contingencies

You may want the following added to the bare bones contract:

1. *Mortgage contingency clause*. This allows you to be legally released from your contract if you can't get the

money, and you will get all of your earnest money back. It is important that the length of the term of the mortgage and the maximum interest rate that you want be spelled out in the contract. If your contract just states mortgage in the amount of $90,000 and the bank turns you down, the seller or someone else can offer to give you a mortgage loan of $90,000 for five years at 18 percent. You would be legally committed to accept it and buy the property (which, of course, you couldn't do) or lose your deposit money. The mortgage contingency clause should also have a cutoff date. Allow yourself plenty of time to get a commitment.

2. *Termite inspection.* In some parts of the country, and especially with attached housing, a "termite bond" must be shown at the closing, showing that the house is treated annually to prevent those pests. Sometimes this is the seller's responsibility, but if not required by law, you will want to pay for an inspection yourself.

3. *Home inspection contingency.* You want your contract subject to an assurance that the plumbing, heating and cooling, electrical systems, and appliances are in working order and that the house is structurally sound.

4. *House delivered vacant.* You probably want the house free for you to move into immediately after closing. If sellers are delayed in leaving for some reason, they often pay a per diem rent to the new owners for the time they stay in that property. Whether you can have an entire two- or three-family home delivered vacant depends on the rent laws in that community and on how they protect renters with a lease.

5. *Sale of existing home*. If you already have a home that is for sale, you might want this clause included in the contract.

6. *The promise of clear title*. You will want a clause in your contract stating that the seller provides title that is free and clear of "clouds on the title."

7. *Personal property*. Everything that is not nailed down (attached to the building) is personal property and not real estate. The best contracts will have a personal property addendum, which lists everything included and not included in the sale. Both the buyer and seller should sign that page.

8. *Subject to buyer's review of (name of community) covenants*. You will want to be sure you can live with the homeowners' association regulations—if you are buying into a community with such an association— before you agree to purchase that home.

9. *Day of closing inspection*. You should inspect the property on the day of the closing, before that transfer takes place, to ensure that everything is as it was promised.

10. *Closing costs*. Who pays for what is up to both you and the seller, although some costs are traditionally the buyer's. Everything is negotiable, but specify in the contract who pays for what.

11. *Liability and maintenance*. You might add a line to this clause that reads something like, "Seller agrees to cut grass, maintain landscaping, and provide for snow removal until closing, and to deliver the premises in question in broom-clean condition."

12. *Subject to review by buyer's attorney*. If you are using a lawyer to handle the sale for you, include this clause,

noting that that review will take place within three to five business days of the date of the contract.

Writing the First Check

Most real-estate agents ask that your check be made out to the broker of record in their firm or to the firm name. When you do this, add the words *trustee* or *fiduciary agent* after the broker's or firm's name in order to protect your money. Your check must then be deposited as money held in trust.

Real-estate law in every state provides that this earnest money will be returned to you if the offer is not accepted and a contract to purchase is not entered into. The return may take some time if the check has been deposited in the broker's account, but most realty agents clip the earnest money check to the contract and carry it around until a deal is struck.

An earnest money check is standard procedure when working through a realty agent. Do not, however, give an earnest money check directly to a seller, not ever. If you are dealing with "for sale by owner" sellers who insist upon earnest money before a contract can be executed, write that check to their lawyer or yours, and write fiduciary agent after the lawyer's name. The money will then be held in a trust account until the negotiations are complete, the contract signed, and its contingencies met. If the deal falls apart, you will get it back.

An Additional Deposit

After a contract is signed, you will be expected to hand over a check to your real-estate agent that, when added to your earnest money deposit, will come to 10 percent of the purchase price. That figure is very negotiable. If you have only $10,000 instead of the $20,000 that is 10 percent of a $200,000 house, the sellers may be amenable to accepting that amount. That check is the down payment and is held in escrow until the closing.

If You Change Your Mind about the House

What happens if you want to scrap your purchase plans after you have signed a contract? Well, your "subject to a lawyer's review" contingency clause can let you off the hook. He or she is likely to find something that does not sit well with you. Or you might not meet one of the contingencies of the contract. For example, you may find the inspection report too negative and say that you do not want the problems of that particular house.

However, after all contingencies have been met, the contract is legal and binding. Your only recourse is the mercy of the sellers, and they may have none. Or they might let you out of the contract but keep your $500 or $1,000 earnest money. (To try to get that sum returned would cost you more in legal fees than the money at issue.) A sympathetic seller could also give you back your earnest money if he or she is able to sell the house quickly to another buyer.

Back to Negotiating: The Counteroffer

The counteroffer is the seller's response to your initial bid. Sometimes it names the actual amount they want for the property but not usually. Most sellers still have some room in their first-response prices, even when they say, "Not a penny less." You now must work toward a meeting of the minds.

In your negotiating diary, record your first offer, its terms, and its contingencies. When you get the counteroffer, record not only its facts and figures but also what the agent says the sellers said. Do they want a quick closing? Is this their bottom price? Are they anxious to sell? Do not take a word of what you hear as gospel truth, though. In negotiating, you must always keep testing for what is "real," and you must never drive anyone into a corner from which there is no escape. The counteroffer is usually returned to you on your original offer form, with numbers crossed out and new numbers written in and initialed.

Your second offer should not be your top dollar, but it should approach your market value estimate. Have the agent write out a whole new offer form. Do not work with scratched-out figures and initials on the old sheet, since this only confuses people.

Add to your negotiating diary the facts of this second offer and any asides that are mentioned by anyone. Keeping such a written account of who said what and when may well prevent arguments, misunderstandings, and denials later. It will also give you a chance to review what happened.

At each step of the bidding, mention to your real-estate agent something to the effect that of course you like and want the house, but it does need kitchen remodeling, or you really wanted a two-car not a one-car garage. You want her to know—and relay to the sellers—that you are not so committed to this house that you will pay anything to own it. There are other homes out there that could suit you, too.

Secrets of Successful Negotiating

Here is how to cleverly navigate the back and forth over price between you and the seller.

- *Know a property's value.* There is nothing more important to successfully buying and selling real estate than knowing the market.

- *Be flexible.* Do not lose a property that you really want over a few dollars a month, which is what financing an extra $500 in sale price would cost you.

- *Never show your hand.* Do not tell anyone, especially not your agent, what you will do next. Act as if the offer you are making will be accepted.

- *Ask for concessions as you increase your bid.* Each time you increase your offering price, ask for something more. That can be almost anything you see: chandeliers, draperies, carpeting, appliances, lawn mowers and garden equipment, lawn furniture, and sometimes even living room or dining room furniture.

- *Use the closing date in your negotiations.* Try to find out early in the game what the sellers want. Compare the seller's needs to yours. How flexible can you afford to be? With your original low offer, name a closing date that is not likely to be to the seller's liking. As you make responses to their counter-offers, you can increase the bid by very little cash but sweeten the deal by moving the proposed closing date into line with the seller's needs. It is almost always worth money.

- *Use financing in your negotiations.* If you plan to pay cash for your home or if you have been preapproved by a mortgage lender, use your strong financial position as a negotiating tool.

- *Keep emotion out of negotiating.* Love the house you are negotiating for, but try not to fall head over heels for it. There are other houses that are just as good—and maybe better.

- *Know when to stop negotiating.* Some deals just cannot be made. If your sellers are not ready to sell at a reasonable price, start looking at other homes.

chapter ten

The House Inspection

One of the contingencies of a sale should be a house inspection by someone you designate, with the results of that evaluation satisfactory to you. House inspections can cost anywhere from $150 to over $500, with the average running about $250. Call a professional only after you have made an offer to buy, that offer has been accepted, and you have signed a sales contract.

An inspector's job is to bring to light any important problems with the house—disasters already there or those about to happen. You might still buy the house, but you can use the inspection report to negotiate for a lower price and/or repairs or replacements. A house inspector also will help you become acquainted with the property that is about to become yours.

When you make your initial phone call to an inspector, ask whether he or she actually goes on the roof and, if possible, gets into the crawl space under the house. Some do these checks as a matter of course, others charge extra, and still others will not go closer to a roof than standing in the driveway, looking up and jotting down impressions from there.

Also, testing for radon and asbestos, well-water contamination, or termites usually costs more than a flat inspection fee. The home inspector/inspection service might, in fact, direct you to someone else for those reports, perhaps to an individual or company that specializes in certain problem areas of a house, particularly environmental hazards.

It is important to learn just what you will be getting for your inspection fee. There is no one "inspection report." Each individual or company has its own form. If possible, look at a sample report.

Ask whether the inspection company carries any type of liability insurance to cover any damage to the house created by the inspector during his or her tour or major defects the house inspector does not catch. How long will the inspection take? A general inspection can run about an hour and a half; a more detailed look that runs two hours plus is likely to cost more. The house inspector, incidentally, should not comment about the wisdom of your buying a particular house, even if you ask (don't bother asking).

When You Inspect a House

Before calling in the pros, do your own inspection. In so doing, you may be able to avoid the aggravation of making a bid on a house, hiring an inspector, and then learning that the house is not worth your investment or that it will cost a fortune in repair bills to bring it up to par.

On your second, or even third, visit to a house, you should get down to the nitty gritty and really look at it. On this visit, wear old clothes and bring the following items with you: a flashlight with a bright beam, a yardstick or tape measure, a marble or small ball (to check the evenness of floors), a pocketknife or ice pick, and a pad and pencil. The following sections will give you an idea of what you should be looking for.

The Foundation

Look for large cracks in the foundation walls that can be seen from both inside and outside the basement. A house with a serious settling problem will have doors and windows that bind and diagonal cracks in the wallboard or plaster, especially above doors and windows. Hairline cracks in the slab that are visible as you walk around outside are not usually a cause for alarm.

The Crawl Space

A wet crawl space can cause joists to rot and can send harmful ground vapors up into the house, causing mildew and dampness. Look for standing water on the ground, especially near the walls and in the corners. Poke at beams with an ice pick. The pick should not sink into the wood; that could be a sign of termites or dry rot. Also look for rodents' nests; rodents love the darkness of crawl spaces.

The Basement

A dry basement is least likely to pose problems. Some basement dampness (as opposed to standing water) is often due to condensation and can be corrected with a dehumidifier.

Seepage from outside ground water is a much more serious problem and can undermine the structural soundness of a house. First, check for water in the corners. If you see some, it may be due to the faulty positioning of a downspout. However, such puddles could be the result of a collection of ground water around the footings, a serious problem that can cause uneven settling. If you see water, suspicious stains, or a newly repainted floor and cracks in the foundation walls, you might want to get the advice of a professional inspector quickly.

Beware also of stains on the basement walls. If you see yellowish brown markings at the same level all around the basement, it is probably dried moisture and is likely to be the high-water mark. That basement does flood or has flooded! Overall, be wary of newly painted walls in a basement area.

Termites

Look for evidence of wood decay and dry rot around the exterior of the house and while you are in the basement. That evidence can take the form of a tunnel-like line running in the problem area. The house does not have to be constructed of wood, either. Use your ice pick in areas where you think you see some evidence of termites. Problems exist if your blade slips into the wood or if you encounter a spongy rather than a solid resistance.

The Working Systems

These systems—electrical, heating, and plumbing—are best handled by professionals. Still, there are some points even a novice can check.

You can find out whether or not the wiring is adequate by looking around the house. If there is a dishwasher, clothes washer and dryer, a few television sets, an electrical stove and oven, central air conditioning, and a computer or two, you can be reasonably certain that wiring is not a problem. Be sure there are enough outlets. Too many appliances and gadgets plugged into extension cords is a sign that the outlet supply is inadequate. Try the light switches. Check to be sure the doorbell rings.

Does the heating system provide enough heat? How much does it cost to run? Ask the owner of the house for the heating bills for the previous winter and the name of the fuel supplier. Then call the oil or utility company and ask what a typical bill for a house of your square footage would have been for the previous winter. Do the same with central air conditioning.

What about the plumbing? You can examine the condition of exposed pipes, but an inspector will likely know more than you about their condition. Old iron pipes or lead fittings could need replacement. Also, be sure to run water from faucets and to flush toilets. Is the water clear or rusty? Look for leaks, low water pressure, and drains that empty too slowly.

Radon and Lead Paint

You've probably read about these problems over the last few years. They can still be serious concerns for some house hunters. Radon is a colorless, odorless gas that came to public attention a decade or so ago. Radon testing is still a routine part of most home purchases. High radon levels can usually be corrected, and remediation arranged before the closing. Most house inspection firms will do radon checks. If yours does not, ask your real-estate agent who in the area does.

Lead-based paint is present in most houses built before 1950. If ingested, it can be very harmful to children, causing brain damage and even death. The federal government has explanations and guidelines for covering this problem. Call your local Housing Authority and/or Health Department.

Calling in the Pros

Once you have some idea of the workings of the house that interests you, you can now call in a professional. Perhaps you know a home remodeler in your town or an engineer who does house inspections. Those folks can be fine, if you are very sure they are qualified to look at every area of a house. There are home inspection companies, too; some of them are local franchises of nationwide concerns.

Be certain your inspector can be objective and owes no allegiance to a real-estate agency or company you might later choose to do repair work on that property. Your best bet is to hire someone who has a contractor's license or experience in residential construction. An engineer might be able to give you advice on repairs and new installations that a house inspection service cannot and is not required to, but you are likely to pay more for the engineer's services.

After the inspection, you should be given a typed report, and quickly. Most companies will have this document in the mail to you in a few days.

Evaluating What You and a Home Inspector Find

Following are some aids to help you determine whether to buy or walk away from a house.

Red lights:

- Unsafe or inadequate drinking water
- A nonfunctioning or malfunctioning private sewer system (septic tank or cesspool)
- Location in a flood plain
- Uneven settling or a buckling foundation
- Uncontrollable basement water problems

Yellow lights:

- Peeling, cracking, or bubbling exterior paint
- A roof almost in need of repairs
- Deteriorating gutters and downspouts

- Leaks in the roof at the flashings
- Excessive moisture in the attic due to poor ventilation or inadequate insulation
- Pests (termites, bats, mice, squirrels, or roaches)
- Inadequate electrical service
- Inadequate insulation
- Plumbing pipes or fixtures in need of repair or replacement
- Leaks around the bathtub or from under a shower stall
- Windows in need of repair or replacement

Green lights:

- An aged or inadequate water heater
- Nonworking appliances (built-in ranges, ovens, dish-washers, etc.)
- Hairline settling cracks in the foundation
- Leaky faucets
- Dirt, grime, and eyesore decorating

chapter eleven

The Closing

What actually happens at the closing? Essentially, a sizable amount of papers are shifted from one party to another for signature. And you pay a fairly sizable amount of costs. Following is a common closing protocol, assuming you will take part in the closing "ceremony."

As soon as it is possible to do so, your lawyer's secretary calls and tells you what your closing expenses will be. If she does not, by all means call that office and ask. The secretary will give you a specific figure and ask you to bring in a cashier's check in that amount, made out to the lawyer. You pay the lawyer for all the expected charges, and from your money, he or she makes disbursements. That is practical, because the money will be paid out in so many different directions. Also, bills for various services needed for the closing will be sent to your lawyer for payment by you at the closing. It would be wise to keep several hundred dollars in your checking account, though, in the unlikely event something else pops up. (If you do not have a lawyer, your mortgage lender will apprise you of settlement costs.)

Closing costs can run as high as 6 percent of the sale price of the home. Costs depend on what the lender charges, what the custom is in your community and your part of the country, what you have already paid before the settlement, and what fees you have negotiated with the sellers for them to pay. The following sections show what you might expect to pay before you truly own your home. Exact figures for most of these charges aren't given because they vary.

Mortgage-Related Charges

- *Loan origination fee.* This fee covers processing your mortgage, stated as a percentage of the loan or as a flat fee.
- *Loan discount or points.* The buyer usually pays the points, but sometimes the seller does. And sometimes there are no points charged.
- *Appraisal fee.* This is usually paid by the buyer but can sometimes be paid by the seller, if both agree. The appraisal charge is sometimes included in the mortgage insurance application fee.
- *Credit report fee.* This fee can also be paid when making a written loan application rather than at the closing.
- *Lender's inspection fee.* This is applicable to new-home buyers. Representatives of the lender must make several inspections at various stages of the building process.
- *Mortgage insurance application fee.* This fee covers the processing costs for applying for private mortgage insurance (PMI).
- *Assumption fee.* This covers the processing work involved in assuming a loan.

Lender-Related Charges

- *Interest*. Interest on their loan for the period of time between the closing date and the date the first scheduled loan payment is due is usually paid by the buyers at the closing.
- *Mortgage insurance premium*. The initial premium is often paid in advance, at the request of the lender. It can cover several months or be a full year's premium.
- *Homeowner's insurance premium*. Your lender could require a first check for this policy.
- *Hazard insurance premium*. If it has been determined that your home is in an area calling for some type of hazard insurance (flood protection, for example), the lender will require proof of payment of the first year's insurance premium at the closing.

Reserve (Escrow) Funds to Be Deposited with the Lender

- *Hazard insurance*. Some lenders require that a certain amount of money toward the next year's premium on hazard insurance be on reserve.
- *Private mortgage insurance*. A part of this premium may be placed in a reserve account rather than being paid in advance at the closing.
- *Real-estate taxes*. This can be a hefty charge of several hundred dollars. Most lenders require a regular monthly payment to the reserve account in your name for city and/or county property taxes. They may also call for an amount of up to six months' taxes to be paid at the closing and held in an escrow account.

- *Special assessments*. Like the tax escrow account, these monies are held in escrow to make payments due either annually or at intervals throughout the year. If you have a clean credit record, ask the lender if you can pay those fees yourself, directly. He or she might say yes!

Charges for Title Services

This is an important, but little known, area of homeowning. Title services ensure that you truly do become the owner of the property you are buying and have written proof of that ownership. There are several fees, of course, in connection with the process of gaining title.

- *Title search, title examination, and title insurance binder*. The latter is sometimes called a "commitment to insure." These are charges made for title search and guarantee services.
- *Title insurance*. This policy protects against any defects in the title that may be discovered after the transfer of ownership has been conveyed.

Other Settlement Charges

- *Settlement or closing fee*. This amount goes to the closing agent. Whether the buyers or the sellers pay it can be negotiated before the contract is signed.
- *Document preparation*. This is a final preparation of legal papers for which you may also be charged.
- *Notary fee*. This fee is paid to a licensed notary public to authenticate the execution of certain applicable documents.

- *Attorney's fee.* If a lawyer is required by the lender, the fee will appear on the Uniform Settlement Statement. If you have engaged an attorney to represent you for this purchase, his or her charge will be a separate bill to you.
- *Government recording and transfer fees.* Charges for legally recording the new deed and mortgage are usually paid by the buyer.
- *Survey.* This is often required by the lender and paid by the buyer.
- *Termite inspection.* Sometimes required by the lender or local custom or law, this bill is usually paid to those rendering that service in advance of the closing, but you must show proof that the service has been provided.
- *Broker's commission.* If you have made an agreement with a buyer's broker, his or her fee will be due at the closing.

Chores for Closing Day

Arrange to have the electric and water meters read the morning of the closing, and then have an account for those utilities set up in your name. Do not wait until the last minute to make these arrangements.

If the house is heated by oil, have the oil company measure what is left in the house the day before closing, if that is agreeable to the seller. Sellers usually charge buyers for any sizable amount of remaining oil when title changes hands. If gas is the fuel, have the meter read on the day of the closing so that the bill for that usage can be sent to the seller, and have a new account opened in your name.

If possible, inspect the property on the morning of the closing. Make a list of any problems or questions that can be raised at the closing. If there has been water damage, for instance, from a pipe that burst after you last saw the property, you are entitled to have something knocked off the sale price or to have the seller write you a check for the estimated cost of repair.

Homeowner's Insurance

Home insurance is one part of the closing ingredients—along with mortgage and property taxes—that will stay with you for the duration of time you live in your new home. While most of the closing documents and receipts can be filed away somewhere in your home, never to be heard from again, you will have to give some thought to insurance each year.

Lenders will not even consider offering you a mortgage if you do not have homeowner's insurance from day one. You will be required to make payments for as long as your home is in their portfolio. With many lenders, your mortgage payment will include homeowner's insurance and sometimes property taxes. If you pay that insurance on your own and let your policy lapse, the insurance company will send a copy of the cancellation to both you and your lender. Your lender could start foreclosure proceedings if the coverage is not reinstated, and quickly.

A basic homeowner's policy protects your home, shrubbery, trees, and outside structures from nearly a dozen perils, including fire, theft, vandalism, lightning, and windstorms. A broad policy adds another seven or so items, including protection against damage from frozen pipes, falling objects, and sprinkler systems—virtually everything but war, nuclear accident, floods, and earthquakes.

The standard homeowner's policy consists of coverage for 100 percent of the replacement value of your home (80 percent replacement is the least you should consider). It is important that you secure replacement coverage, which is what it would cost to rebuild the home at today's prices.

You should also have coverage for your personal belongings, with separate floaters for pieces of art or jewelry, as well as liability coverage to protect you if someone is injured in your home or on your property. The policy should not cover the land. After all, you can, in all likelihood, build on it again. Similarly, the foundation is likely to be there following almost any calamity, so do not insure that either.

You might also give some thought to an umbrella policy. This liability protection has a separate policy that picks up where both your homeowner's and automobile policies leave off. Umbrellas can cost about $150 to $200 annually for $1 million of coverage, going up to $250 to $300 for as much as $10 million.

There are special insurance packages for still other calamities. The three most common are flood, hurricane, and earthquake coverage.

Flood Insurance

Flood protection does not come with a standard homeowner's policy. If you live in a flood-prone area, your lender will require you to purchase this special protection. It runs about $150 to $200 for $85,000 worth of coverage each year.

Flood insurance is offered by the federal government through the National Flood Insurance Program, administered by the Federal Emergency Management Agency (FEMA). If you have any questions, call that office at (800) 638-6620. You can purchase a flood insurance policy through most insurance offices.

Hurricane Coverage

A standard homeowner's policy provides coverage for windstorm damage, but if you live in a particularly dangerous locale for those storms, you can purchase a special windstorm insurance policy through an independent company or a statewide insurance pool.

Earthquake Coverage

Earthquake insurance can be secured for a high fee and a high deductible. You can secure an earthquake policy from your homeowner's insurance agent, who must offer earthquake protection to Californians.

Keeping Track of Your Policy

Check your coverage annually, and update it periodically if housing prices rise and the replacement cost of your home goes up. If you have bought a fixer-upper and have done extensive—and expensive—remodeling or if you have purchased new furnishings, check your insurance package. An inflation guard policy that automatically adjusts your plan each year to cover rises in building costs covers only inflation, so do not rely on that for total security.

index

115